A GLOSSARY OF
APPLIED LINGUISTICS

A Glossary of
Applied Linguistics

Alan Davies

LEA LAWRENCE ERLBAUM ASSOCIATES, PUBLISHERS
2005   Mahwah, New Jersey   London

First published 2005 by
EDINBURGH UNIVERSITY PRESS LTD
22 George Square
Edinburgh

First published in North America by
LAWRENCE ERLBAUM ASSOCIATES, INC.
10 Industrial Avenue
Mahwah, New Jersey 07430

Lawrence Erlbaum Associates, Inc., Publishers
10 Industrial Avenue
Mahwah, New Jersey 07430

Library of Congress Cataloging-in-Publication data

Davies, Alan, Ph. D.
    A glossary of applied linguistics / Alan Davies.
        p. cm.
    Includes bibliographical references and index.
    ISBN 0-8058-5728-1 (alk. paper) – ISBN 978-0-8058-5729-0
    (pbk. : alk. paper)
        1. Applied linguistics–Terminology. I Title.
    P129.D368 2005
    418'.001'4–dc22

Contents

Acknowledgements

Writing a single authored glossary of applied linguistics has advantages and disadvantages. The advantages are, it is to be hoped, coherence and a unified perspective. The disadvantages are the lack of expertise across so wide-ranging a field and the inevitable solitariness of the task. But, as Dr Johnston's old friend, Mr Edwards, remarked: 'cheerfulness was always breaking in', encouraged as I have been by Catherine Elder and by Sarah Edwards of EUP, and delighted as I have also been by my grandchildren, George, Alice and Hannah.

Preface

Acronyms in the glossary are normally explained. Some that are not and are made use of several times are:

Lx   Source language
Ly   Target language
L1   First language
L2   Second language – any second language since for an individual it may be the second, third or fourth

Terms highlighted within entries will be found as head-words elsewhere in the Glossary.

The text refers to a number of scholars. These include:

Anderson, Benedict
Bakhtin, Mikhail
Barth, Frederik
Bernstein, Basil
Bormuth, John R.
Brass, Paul
Brumfit, Christopher
Carroll, John B.
Chomsky, Noam
Corder, S. Pit
Cummins, Jim
Fairclough, Norman
Ferguson, Charles

Firth, John R.
Foucault, Michel
Francis, Nelson
Garfinkel, Harold
Guttman, Louis
Halliday, Michael A. K.
Hymes, Dell
Johnson, Samuel
Jones, Daniel
Kachru, Braj
Labov, William
Lakoff, George
Lambert, Wallace E.
Lantolf, James
Le Page, Robert
Likert, Renis
Malinowski, Bronislaw
Marx, Karl
Osgood, Charles E.
Perren, George E.
Phillipson, Robert
Piaget, Jean
Sapir, Edward
Sapon, Stanley M.
Saussure, Ferdinand de
Selinker, Larry
Spolsky, Bernard
Thurstone, Louis Leon
Voloshinov, Valentin
Vygotsky, Lev
Weir, Cyril
Whorf, Benjamin Lee
Widdowson, Henry G.

Introduction

The urgent question mark against applied linguistics is just what is its source, what exactly is being applied. If the interpretation of applied linguistics is very narrow so that what is being applied is only linguistics, then because linguistics, like other theoretical disciplines, deals with idealisations, it appears to have very little to say about the language-related problems in what we call the real world. If applied linguistics is interpreted very broadly, then it must concern itself with everything to do with language. Neither position is tenable. Linguistics, it seems, must play an important role in applied linguistics but by no means the only role. Applied linguistics must also draw on psychology, sociology, education, measurement theory and so on.

It may be that we shall gain a clearer picture of the nature of applied linguistics if we turn our attention away from the source (what applied linguistics draws on) to its target (what applied linguistics equips you to do). The target clearly cannot be anything and everything to do with language. Corder's solution (Corder 1973) was to focus on language teaching, widely interpreted, and therefore including, for example, speech therapy, translation and language planning. Such narrowing of the target still makes sense today, which is why most of the entries in this glossary have some connection with language teaching. Our reasoning is that it remains true that many of those who study applied linguistics have been and will continue to be involved at some level in language teaching, which is, after all, the largest profession involved in language studies. This is not to say that once a language teacher, always one: some, perhaps many, of those who engage with applied linguistics move on to research, administration and so on. But for the purposes of the glossary we have found it helpful to provide ourselves with this constraint on what it is we claim as applied linguistics. What that means is that, while we accept Brumfit's definition – 'A working definition of applied linguistics will then be the theoretical and empirical investigation of real-world problems in which language is a central issue' (Brumfit 1997: 93) – in this glossary we avoid the danger of the 'science of everything' position by targeting language teaching. At the same time we recognise that the world of language learning and teaching is not an artificial world but one that must engage every day with Brumfit's real-world problems, involving success and failure, ability and disability, ethical, cultural and gender issues, technology and lack of resources, the difficult and the simple, the child and the adult.

References

Brumfit, Christopher, 'How applied linguistics is the same as any other science', *International Journal of Applied Linguistics*, 1997, 7/1: 86–94.

Corder, S. Pit, *Introducing Applied Linguistics*, Harmondsworth: Penguin, 1973.

A

AAAL American Association of Applied Linguistics, the professional organisation of American applied linguists. Membership is open: there are no restrictions on entry based on qualifications, experience or nationality. AAAL is now the largest **applied linguistics** association and attracts large number of applied linguists world-wide to its annual conferences. Its view of applied linguistics is both eclectic and comprehensive.

AAVE African American Vernacular English, also termed, at various times, Black English and **Ebonics**. AAVE represents (or is said to represent) the **dialect** (or, as more militant commentators would say, the **language**) of Black Americans. Undoubtedly, AAVE represents a dialect of English that is widely used among Black Americans in informal spoken interactions. The issue that is un-resolved is whether this dialect should be officially recognised as the medium of **education** for young Black Americans (see **world Englishes**), the argument being that young Black Americans are more likely to develop cognitively if taught in their own dialect and if that dialect is accorded official status (see **BICS**). Such an argument remains contentious and is not accepted by all (or perhaps by most) Black Americans, although some linguists do support it.

ability Current capacity to perform an act. **Language teaching** is concerned with a subset of cognitive or mental abilities and therefore with skills underlying behaviour (for example, reading ability, speaking ability) as well as with potential ability to learn a language (**aptitude**). Ability has a more general meaning than terms such as **achievement**, attainment, aptitude, **proficiency**, while capacity and **knowledge** are sometimes used as loose synonyms. Ability is difficult to define and to investigate, perhaps because it cannot be observed directly. See also **language testing**.

academic discourse The use of language at an advanced level of education to discuss cognitively difficult concepts for analysis and for argument. One of the more robust language uses which are grouped under the heading of **LSP**, it readily lends itself to **proficiency** teaching and testing. It seems likely that what distinguishes academic discourse from general discourse is difficulty, itself attributable to precision of concept formation and development.

accent Features of the speech signal that identify individuals as belonging to certain groups which may be geographical or **social class**-based. While a particular **dialect** may be spoken in a variety of accents, the reverse is not the case. **Education** and status are more closely associated with a standard dialect and more leeway is permitted to accent variation. However, in spoken interaction accent is very salient and undoubtedly influences interlocutors' judgements of one another. Perhaps because accent is more resistant to change than dialect (hence foreign accents) and more easily identified with origin and **identity**, there is little emphasis today on using education to change accent. Even so, it does seem that one of the effects of education (however indirect) is to bring about some **accommodation** towards a **norm** with **prestige**.

accommodation The tendency for all interlocutors to move their own **language use** closer to one another's for ease of understanding and for greater solidarity, both linguistically and attitudinally. **Power** imbalance seems to affect the degree of accommodation, whereby the less powerful make greater accommodation when interacting with the more powerful. However, neither relationship nor power is straightforward and it is important to recognise different dimensions of power, which can include strength of **personality**.

accuracy We may distinguish traditional and critical approaches to accuracy. The traditional view is that there is a correct way to use the rules and especially the **grammar** of Language X. The purpose of **education**, therefore, both L1 and L2, is seen to be the inculcation of those rules, especially at the higher levels of education, in writing. The approach of **critical applied linguistics** seems to be to reject the assumption of **norms**, which would imply that accuracy is not relevant. However, it is unclear whether critical applied linguistics would go that far since, without norms, **language** would be difficult to learn and to teach. The critical applied linguistic concern with the need to recognise where **power** in language resides and therefore who decides what is accurate seems at odds with its assumption that norms are not important.

achievement Tests that measure progress on a known syllabus are called achievement (or attainment) tests. They are not concerned with predicting future success or with assessing whether the level reached by a candidate is sufficient to carry out various non-language tasks (such as being a tour operator, studying medicine in the medium of the language): that is the role of the **language proficiency test**. The purpose of the achievement test is to determine whether the language material that has been taught has been learned.

acquisition Naturalistic learning of a **language**, whether L1 or L2. Language acquisition is therefore to be distinguished from **language learning**, which refers to the formal method(s) of language acquisition. The terms are, however, often used interchangeably.

acrolect The variety that has the most **prestige** in a **dialect** continuum, followed by the **mesolect** and at the bottom the **basilect**.

act of identity All **speech acts** are said by Le Page to represent a speaker's **identity** in a particular **context**. The assumption is that individuals have a verbal repertoire which allows them to choose how to indicate the identity they wish to claim.

action research **Research** (in, for example, the classroom or the hospital ward) which offers engagement, commitment and observation in place of the rigid controls expected of, for example, **positivist** research. Whether action research deserves to be regarded as research is a moot point. But tell that to the anthropologists.

adjacency pair A basic organisational sequence in conversation. Adjacency pairs are formulaic type utterances in conversation in which the first part of the pair by A triggers the second part by B (for example: How are you today/I'm very well, thank you). Failure to complete the adjacency pair is infelicitous and indicative of either a lack of proficiency or deliberate deviousness. See also **CA, ritualised routines.**

advertising A paid-for form of non-personal communication about an organisation, product, service or idea by an identified sponsor. Both advertising and **propaganda** are said to be one-to-many forms of communication.

African American Vernacular English see **AAVE**

age factors Age is a determinant in **language acquisition,** in that for **native speaker** control in Language X to be achieved, language acquisition must normally take place before the critical or sensitive age. Age also seems to affect **language learning** (as it does other aspects of learning) in that with the gradual effluxion of time, language learning becomes more difficult. Furthermore, age also has a negative effect on already acquired and learnt languages. Individuals tend in later life to lose second languages, although this may be (as with community languages) a function more of lack of use than of age. Age also has a negative effect on L1, whereby immediate recall, especially for names, is less automatic with increasing age. See also **critical period, SLAR.**

AILA Association Internationale de Linguistique Appliquée, known in English as the International Association of Applied Linguistics. AILA has been in existence since 1960 and brings together representatives from its thirty-plus national associations in an international committee to promote research and development in applied linguistics. AILA organises a peripatetic triennial congress and is associated with several journals, including the *AILA Review.* See also **AAAL, BAAL.**

ALAA Applied Linguistics Association of Australia.

alphabetic A system of written script in which there is a
direct correspondence between **graphemes** and
phonemes. As such, it is the most economical of all
systems of writing. Languages vary in the degree of their
grapheme–phoneme correspondence. Spanish is very
regular while English is very irregular. Hence the many
arbitrary spelling rules of written English children and
non-native speakers must learn.

alphabetisation A necessary stage towards the acquisition in
Language X of literacy. Much practised by missionary
organisations such as SIL, alphabetisation provides a
written formulation for the spoken language. Such
formulation is indicative of the conventional nature of
language, in that different alphabetisations are perfectly
possible for the same language and may indeed be in
conflict with one another. For example, in Fiji different
missionaries advocated their own preferred formulation,
to some extent influenced by a contrastive linguistics,
based on their own mother tongue. See also **contrastive
analysis**.

American Association of Applied Linguistics see **AAAL**

American English A distinction needs to be made between
American Englishes, those varieties of English as an L1
spoken in different parts of the USA; and American
English, the standard version of the dialect. While
American English and **British English** (and **Australian
English**, etc.) are mutually intelligible, each of them has
certain distinct standard features which are attested to
and described in **dictionaries** and style guides and appear
in publishers' usage. At the beginning of the twenty-first

century, American English is by far the most influential of these national standards and seems likely for some time to come to exercise a globalising influence on the other standards. See also **language standards.**

American Sign Language see **deaf education**

analysis of variance A statistical technique which examines the interrelationship among a group of **variables** (for example, **social class, gender, age,** L1, second language proficiency) and in so doing estimates the influence on the **criterion** of each variable and of their joint influence.

anthropological linguistics In the USA, linguistics and anthropology grew up together. Linguistics was to some extent (perhaps because of the interest in American Indian languages) viewed as a branch of anthropology, a development also found in Australia. This influence has been instrumental in the interactions between anthropology (and sociology) and linguistics, leading to the growth of **sociolinguistics,** ethnolinguistics and **conversation analysis,** and to the continuing interest among many American applied linguists in **culture:** hence the development of ideas about **communicative competence.**

aphasias While age has a normal developmental influence on an individual's language control, traumas of various kinds, including head injuries and strokes, can damage the brain and cause an aphasia. Depending on the location and extent of the injury, this may cause loss of capacity to speak, wholly or in part, to write and to remember. See also **clinical linguistics, speech pathology.**

applied linguistics Definitions such as 'the exploration of real-world problems in which language is important' are common, but it is necessary to point out that among those professing applied linguistics the focus of attention differs. Some, more interested perhaps in theoretical linguistic issues, focus on the language; others, perhaps more interested in social issues and their possible amelioration, focus on the problems themselves.

applied linguistics research Research in applied linguistics is no different from research in other disciplines, both theoretical and applied. There is, however, one difference, a difference that pertains to all applied areas. This is that many of its research areas are motivated by institutional needs and practical requirements. What this means is that the research paradigm which, in the theoretical disciplines, may be prompted by the paradigm currently in favour, in the applied disciplines is prompted by a social demand which itself may draw on the current paradigm.

aptitude see **language aptitude**

artificial languages The canonical cases of artificial languages can be found in those nineteenth-century inventions such as Esperanto and Idaho which had as their aim greater understanding among people and nations. But a case can be made for a more widespread definition whereby all language interventions result in non-natural language outcomes. Thus simplified languages (for example, Basic English), but also, to an extent, standard languages which are brought about by deliberate interventions and non-natural choices of lexis and grammar. See also **simplification, standards.**

ASL American Sign Language. See **deaf education.**

assessment Often used interchangeably with **testing** and/or examining, but also used as a superordinate encompassing testing, examining and evaluation. Assessment concerns the measurement of **proficiency** and of potential (or **aptitude**) in terms of the progress of **language learning**. Assessment, both formal and informal, has always been important in **language teaching**, but in recent years the expansion of education provision, the increasing concern for accountability and the consequent audit have made assessment even more influential. See also **curriculum, syllabus**.

Association Internationale de Linguistique Appliquée see **AILA**

attitude An individual's attitude influences his or her approach to members of other language groups and to his or her own first and second language. Where, as is often the case, such attitudes are negative, changing them is hard, but it does seem that bringing them into the open may help make them more positive or at least less negative. Lambert and colleagues at McGill University in Montreal pioneered various methodologies for the study of language attitudes, notably the **matched guise technique**.

audience Learners and aspirant writers are encouraged to attend to their audience, to write or speak to them, to have them in mind, in other words to make their discourse and its analysis more context sensitive. Of course, the more context sensitive the performance, the less likely it is to have a wider application and so to appeal to larger audiences.

audiolingual Thought to be the breakthrough in teaching **methodology** in the 1960s and 1970s because it enabled the language teacher and learner greater access to realistic language contexts. Looking back now in the early 2000s, it is easy to see that what audiolingual methodology was doing was to capitalise on recent hardware developments such as the portable tape recorder. It seems possible that a generation from now we will be making similar disparaging remarks about the computer and its software.

Australian English Like **American English, Australian English** has its own distinctive lexis. It seems unlikely that its **grammar** is different from that of **British English;** indeed its differences, except in **vocabulary,** are quite minor; and even in vocabulary what Australian English does is to add and supplement rather than replace. A curious and unexplained difference between the Australian and the American varieties is that while there are regional varieties of spoken American English, there appear to be no regional or local accentual differences in the English spoken in Australia. See also **language varieties.**

authenticity A somewhat heretical requirement (in the 1970s and 1980s) for language **teaching materials** that became associated with **communicative competence** developments. The idea seems to have been that for the best results, learners needed to be placed in as naturalistic an environment as possible. The rationale, which was rarely made explicit, was that the best **language learning** takes place among young children learning their L1, and therefore what second language teaching should do is, as far as possible, to replicate that environment. The deliberate pursuit of authenticity contained its own failure, since by definition authenticity must be non-deliberate. No doubt informal **SLL** could use authenticity, but only if it remained informal and therefore beyond the reaches of planning and organising.

B

BAAL British Association of Applied Linguistics. BAAL has been in existence since 1967. It sponsors seminars and holds an annual conference. With **AAAL** and **AILA**, it sponsors the leading journal in the field, *Applied Linguistics*. Membership is open; the organisation regards itself as the chief professional body for applied linguists in the UK.

back-channel responses Phatic signals provided by interlocutors to signal that they are attentive to what is being said by their partner(s) in a **conversation**. These responses are in themselves empty of **meaning**, although **CA** has researched them and invested them with differential intent. See also **phatic communion**.

background knowledge (also **background information**) The information that the listener needs in order to be able to understand new information. If the background information is not generally available then the speaker needs to introduce it early in the interaction in order to provide the necessary context for the subsequent new information.

backsliding In **SLL**, the temporary reappearance of features from an earlier stage of the learner's development. The cause is thought to be stress, and when the reason for the stress has been removed, the errors will disappear.

Basic English A modified language, based on English, the purpose being to promote mainly technical communication, hence the name: B(ritish) A(merican) S(cientific) I(nternational) C(ommunication). Invented by C. K. Ogden and I. A. Richards in 1929, it consists of 850 English words selected to cover everyday needs. It has been remarked that in Basic English the **vocabulary** was simplified at the expense of the **grammar**. And even the vocabulary was not quite so simple: the 850 selected words were all headwords, which means that there are very many more based on those headwords. Basic English received early support from political leaders such as Churchill and Roosevelt, but, like artificial languages such as **Esperanto**, it has been regarded by applied linguists as little more than a curiosity, irrelevant to the solution of language problems.

basic interpersonal communication skills see **BICS**

basilect see **acrolect**

behaviourism An all-embracing psychological theory which asserted that all behaviour (and therefore all learning) is a matter of stimulus-response. In **language learning,** this became particularly associated with decontextualised instruction (and tests) which lent themselves to formulaic responses. Behaviourism in psychology was associated with **structuralism** in **linguistics**, which was also largely uninvolved in social contexts. Behaviourism provided the construct for the development of language learning through **audiolingual** instruction, in particular through **language laboratories**. What behaviourism did was to surrender to the exigencies of the hardware its own need for research. But **cognitive development**, it came to be recognised, is more complex and requires

creativity and spontaneity. What behaviourism exemplifies is an object lesson in the need for a range of theoretical explanations of phenomena, not for just one theory.

benchmark A description of where students should be at certain points in following a **syllabus**. The description typically makes use of a **scale** and sets out the expected levels of **performance** on the scale that students should reach as they progress through the system. See also **standards**.

BICS Basic interpersonal communication skills, those interpersonal skills that are necessary to later cognitive development and which can be acquired only in the L1. The BICS-**CALP** distinction has been developed by Jim Cummins but in its extreme version ('No CALP without BICS'), as an argument in favour of **education** only in the L1, it appears untenable.

bilingual education Implies an **education** in more than one language. It is offered in a range of options, from the (Canadian) **immersion** where one language (usually French) takes up the majority of the **curriculum** and English (the L1 of the students in this case) is given a small share of time, through the more balanced programmes where Language X and Language Y are given fairly equal amounts of curriculum time (for example, Welsh and English in some schools in Wales), to the foreign language instruction situation where the second/foreign language is given a small share of time. Bilingual education is indeed a broad church and while all the views we have cited may be regarded as types of bilingual education provision, it is probably the case that the second version is most typical. However, no system (not even Canadian immersion) appears to provide complete ambilingualism (= balanced bilingualism), which may suggest that such a goal is unattainable. Even the provision of double time, whereby each language repeats the content of the other's timetable, does not solve the immersion dilemma, data from which seems to indicate that Canadian anglophone immersion graduates have not internalised the grammatical intuitions of the (French) L1 speaker. This must mean that while full bilingualism can be obtained informally, bilingual education has to be defined in terms of the goal in mind.

bilingualism The state of controlling two languages. The term is a primitive (non-theoretical) in the sense that there are no agreed definitions of control, thus bilingualism extends from the position of the person exposed as a child to two languages (often the father's and the mother's), through the informal acquisition of the non-home **language** from peers, to the formal school learning which itself takes a variety of forms (see **bilingual education**), from the second language as medium to the second language as a foreign language. If bilingualism is extended even further, then, as bidialectalism, it can be said to include the control over two **dialects**, that of the home and that of the locality etc. As such, it seems reasonable, if somewhat absurd, to assert that we are all bilinguals.

biliteracy The state of control of the written language in two codes. The range of positions on the biliteracy continuum is similar to that of **bilingualism**, although in terms of fluency (near-native) it seems likely that advanced bilingualism in the spoken language is easier to achieve than advanced biliteracy. Undoubtedly famous cases are attested of those who write with skill in two languages (for example, Samuel Beckett), but they are probably exceptional. See also **writing**.

Bokmal (originally known as Riksmal) One of the two officially recognised **standard** forms of Norwegian, the other being Nynorsk. Bokmal is closer to Danish, which for centuries was the official language of Norway, while Nynorsk is a standardised combination of a number of Norwegian **dialects**.

Braille A form of alphabetism which uses raised dots on the page to signal the spoken language to unsighted and partially sighted readers. Braille was invented by Louis Braille in 1829 and the first Braille Press was established in Edinburgh in 1891. See also **alphabetisation**.

British Council The para-statal cultural arm of the UK government, the British Council exists to promote Britain overseas, its life, languages and **cultures**. Exchanges of people and ideas are central to its activities and it oversees the attendance in UK higher education of large numbers of overseas students, especially at the graduate level. In the 1960s and 1970s the dissemination of advice on English **language teaching** and **learning** was of major importance to the British Council, and a large cadre of English language officers was deployed to spread good practice in English language teaching world-wide. That initiative is no more. There is less government aid available, and commercial considerations now affect British Council policy and activity.

British English Refers to the **Standard English** employed by schools and public bodies (for example, the BBC, publishers) in the UK. As with **American English**,

Australian English and so on, British English is to be regarded as a **dialect** of English and can therefore be spoken in a variety of **accents**.

British Sign Language see **BSL**

Broca's area That area of the brain (right side) that when damaged (through stroke or accident) leads to a variety of **aphasias**. Through therapy, the patient can learn to compensate in various ways, but damage to Broca's area can never be fully healed. See also **clinical linguistics, speech pathology**.

Brown Corpus A pioneer lexical database, first established at Brown University, where it was inaugurated by Nelson Francis. Beginning as alternatives to **dictionaries**, corpuses are now important in both linguistic and applied linguistic **research**, providing data for language descriptions, language teaching syllabuses and textbooks and as evidence for **testing** linguistic theories. See **corpus linguistics, lexis**.

BSL British Sign Language, the communicative system employed by hearing-impaired people in the UK. It consists of systematic head and face movements and gestures and has been standardised. It appears to be the case that it is acquired from peers and in schools for the deaf. It is not based on **British English** and at the same time is not mutually intelligible with other sign languages, for example American Sign Language.

Bullock Report The report of a government-commissioned report (*A Language for Life*, 1975) referring to the teaching of English in schools in England and Wales. Its originality was in its recommendations for the teaching of a linguistically informed view of **language** in schools.

C

CA Conversation analysis, a study of the **norms** governing interactions between speakers. Aspects of interaction of interest to CA scholars include the relationship between questions and answers and between statements and responses, and the rules for **turn-taking**, for opening and closing a conversation, for interruptions, for overlapping and for changing the topic. Unlike **discourse analysis**, which imposes a top-down grid and theoretical framework (or ideology) in its analysis of texts, CA declares itself theory neutral and operates (again it is claimed) a bottom-up analysis where the data determine the outcome. See also **cross-cultural communication, ethnomethodology**.

CAL Center for Applied Linguistics. Based in Washington, DC, the Center was founded in 1959 by Charles Ferguson with funding from the Ford Foundation. Its mandate was to be a resource base for **ESL**, and to become a national resource for the application of **linguistics** and of new methods generally to the teaching and learning of second languages. CAL has become and remains today a major resource for research and development in ESL, immigrant education, foreign language education, language proficiency assessment, bilingual and vernacular education, refugee education and services, language policy and planning, and cross-cultural communication.

CALL Computer assisted language learning. Computers, like programmed instruction, audio-visual learning and language laboratories, have created interest in different approaches to language learning and teaching. Apart from help with simulating situations of language use, computers have two strengths: speed and distance learning. However, they also have disadvantages: they lend themselves more readily to structural exercises than to more creative opportunities and they still need teacher back-up. Nevertheless, if through sound and visuals their attempts at simulation can be improved, they are likely to make an important contribution to distance language learning and teaching, and even more to distance teaching of applied linguistics.

CALP Cognitive academic language proficiency; the skills that are developed through formal education. Cummins has proposed that CALP can be acquired only after the development of BICS through early education in the first language. This view has been challenged.

case studies A qualitative methodology that makes use of anthropological-type observation of particular situations. Case studies are said to provide rich research data; their downside is that their very particularity makes generalisation difficult. See also qualitative research.

censuses Population censuses are normally carried out at regular intervals, sometimes of five years, more commonly ten. In some cases, census questions about language background and use are included. While such questions as: 'Do you speak/write Language X?' are inevitably flawed by self-report, the accumulation of such data (however flawed) over time permits extrapolation of language trends.

Center for Applied Linguistics see **CAL**

Centre for Information on Language Teaching see **CILT**

child language acquisition Since a **native speaker** of Language X is usually considered to be one who has learnt the language in childhood, the term 'child (or **first**) **language acquisition**' is reserved for **research** into the acquisition process of the first language speaker. It is therefore in contrast with **second language acquisition**, which may focus on **age factors**. Child language acquisition has for long been dominated by a Chomskian paradigm but it looks now as though researchers are employing more eclectic approaches. See also **SLAR**.

CILT The Centre for Information on Language Teaching in London (with a branch in Scotland) developed out of the **British Council**'s English Teaching Information Centre (ETIC), which Perren created in 1964. The heart of both enterprises was a well-stocked **applied linguistics** library; in addition CILT provides support for journals, state-of-the-art reports and seminars. CILT expanded the work of ETIC by taking into account the teaching of foreign languages in the UK; it also limited it by reducing its emphasis on **TEFL** across the world.

classical test theory (also **classical true score measurement theory**) A theory which consists of a set of assumptions about the relationships between actual and observed scores on a test. Traditional item-analysis procedures are based on this theory, which in recent years has been challenged by **IRT** models. These overcome some of the inherent problems with the classical model by expressing the relationship of item difficulty and individual **ability** within a single framework.

classroom discourse The study of **language learning** in the second/foreign language classroom. Since for many (perhaps most) students learning a foreign or second language the teacher is their only source for the **target language, research** on the classroom as a major site for learning makes sense.

clinical linguistics The application of **linguistics** to the analysis of medical conditions involving a language disorder, such as cleft palate, hearing problems or **aphasias**. See also **speech pathology**.

Cloze procedure A testing technique employing the gap-filling procedure developed by Wilson Taylor in the 1950s as a means of assessing the **readability** of newspapers. Cloze has been widely used in proficiency testing and although there are different ways of presentation and of scoring, the most common method still employs random gapping; that is, every fifth, seventh or nth word is deleted and the person being tested must restore the original deleted word.

code mixing Switching between two or more languages within sentences and phrases. Attempts have been made to show that such mixing is systematic, with little success. However, it does seem likely that while the switches may be random, what the act itself means is the projection of a dual identity. Mixing should be distinguished from borrowing: in mixing the speaker has bilingual capacity. Borrowing concerns the intrusion of one language into another through, for example, lexical additions.

code switching The shift in one piece of discourse from one **language** (Language X) to another language (Language

Y). Switching occurs because **code mixing** is available. The location of switching is much researched but remains unclear.

codes The term is used in two related senses. The first is linguistic and implies a systematic linguistic variety, which may be at the **language** level, at the **dialect** level or at the **register** level: thus, German is a code, Schwitzer Deutsch is a code, the German of chemistry textbooks is a code. The second sense is more sociological and is associated with the work of Bernstein and followers. There 'code' is used to distinguish symbolic systems defining **social classes,** for example **elaborated codes** and **restricted codes.** Elaborated codes are said to be **context**-free and therefore more objective and understandable by outsiders. Restricted codes are said to be available only to insiders who must share the cultural assumptions of the in-group for understanding to take place. Bernstein's linking of the two codes to the middle classes (elaborated) and working classes (restricted) met with fierce opposition, but this linking is not essential to his basic argument.

codification The act of describing a language so as to determine a normative **grammar,** lexicon and so on. Codification is commonly the precursor to standardisation. Although it seems possible for there to be an oral tradition of language **norms,** it is usual for the agreed codification of a language, its grammar, its **lexis** (in **dictionary** form) and sometimes manuals of **usage,** to be written down, making it less open to ambiguity.

cognitive academic language proficiency see **CALP**

cognitive development Akin to physical development. Like physical development, cognitive development is reckoned to proceed by stages. One of the best-known psychological models is that of Piaget, who posits three or four stages, the last being that of abstract thinking. Chomskian linguistics modelled its language development sequencing on Piaget's model, but linguistic development, unlike physical and perhaps cognitive development, does appear to depend, at least in part, on input from interlocutors and care-givers and on context.

cognitive psychology see **cognitive development**

coherence The (semantic) relationships among utterances in a **text**, while **cohesion** refers to the grammatical and lexical relationships among the elements of a text. A text that has coherence but lacks cohesion is without signposts; a text that has cohesion but lacks coherence is without **meaning**.

cohesion The grammatical and lexical relationships among the elements of a **text**, while **coherence** refers to the (semantic) relationships among utterances in a text. A text that has cohesion but lacks coherence has no **meaning**; a text that has coherence but lacks cohesion is without signposts.

colloquial A very informal style of speaking. It has links with the sociolinguistic notion of **vernacular**, which, according to Labov, is the style freely used by intimates when they are not being observed.

colonial discourse Refers to the writing (and less to the speaking) of those involved in and affected by colonisation. Colonial **discourse** (for example *Uncle Tom's Cabin*, much of Rudyard Kipling) is uncritical of empire and of colonisation. Such criticism arrives with post-colonialism.

communication The exchange of feelings, ideas etc., thought by some to be the main reason for the existence of **language** and its main task. Communication may be measured in bits, indicating the extent of information being exchanged. But communication is also a term for linguistic interaction and as such does not require the exchange of meaningful **context**, since **phatic communion** may be regarded as an act of communication.

communicative competence The analogue of linguistic competence, the individual's capacity to develop linguistically and become a **native speaker**. Communicative competence was the attempt by Hymes to extend the rational, cognitive model to the social, claiming that **language acquisition** must incorporate systematic learning of social and cultural interaction. It would be more appropriate to speak of **competences**, since communicative competence includes (at least) linguistic competence, discourse competence, **pragmatic competence**, **sociolinguistic competence** and sociocultural competence.

communicative language teaching The paradigm shift (in the UK and elsewhere) in the 1970s to teach and learn languages in **context**, implying that the model for **SLL** and second language teaching must be that of the L1, and therefore attempting to simulate (as far as possible) the spontaneity, **creativity** and needs of the L1 learner. It appears that the ambition was over-reaching; in unskilful hands, communicative language teaching led to a curious replication of rote learning simply because the demands were too high.

communicative language testing The use of language tests that claim to operationalise theories of **communicative competence**. The tests take different forms, depending on which dimensions they choose to emphasise, for example specificity of **context, authenticity** of materials, or the simulation of real-life performance.

communities of practice The term used for professional and work groups etc. that make use of a specialist **code**, for example the language of medicine, the language of accountants, the language of military lawyers. See also **domains, ESP, LSP, register**.

competence Distinguished by Chomsky from **performance** and analogous to the Saussurean **langue**, competence (more accurately linguistic competence) refers to the language capacity that exists in all normal children and that permits the **acquisition** of the contextually based **language** to which the young child is exposed.

complexity Like its opposite, simplicity, complexity is difficult to pin down, dependent as it is on content and the **background knowledge** of the reader/listener. If content is held constant, it is likely that longer sentences, containing several subordinate clauses, will be more complex than simple, one-clause sentences. Similarly, longer or less frequently occurring words are likely to be more complex than shorter, more frequent words. However, things are not quite so straightforward. Our understanding of shorter, frequent words is often confused by ambiguity and homonymy. Take, for example, the word 'hand' in 'He put his hand on the table.' Hand, here, can be disambiguated only by context (= limb, playing cards). Although there is much interest in developing a linguistic complexity index, no independent measure of complexity has yet been agreed. See also **simplification.**

composition writing Compositions are pieces of continuous writing on a given theme. They represent traditional **tasks** at all levels of **education,** but in L1 and L2 teaching are often used as items of assessment. The more formal term **essay** is sometimes used. In North American universities, composition writing is a compulsory Year 1 subject, the rationale being that too little practice has been available in the high school and that writing extended prose compositions helps develop the cognitive skills required in all higher education. See also **academic discourse.**

comprehension A particular (and probably narrower) type of understanding, commonly used to refer to the teaching and **assessment** of **texts.**

computer assisted language learning see **CALL**

concordance A type of **dictionary** giving page references to all the words and phrases in a given **text,** for example the Bible Concordance. Software is now available for preparing concordances electronically. These programs analyse large numbers of texts (known as a **language corpus**) and the results are sometimes used to generate a dictionary.

construct A model (or theory or idea) that the teacher, tester or researcher brings to the project in place. The assumption is that a construct is sufficiently coherent to be falsifiable. See also **validity.**

context The **variables** other than the **language** tokens (individual word occurrences) themselves in which a language event takes place. Context therefore includes background, content, and cultural, physical and inter- locutor relationships etc. Full knowledge of context can render the language of the language event redundant; that is, it becomes phatic. See also **phatic com- munication**.

context of situation A term employed by Firth and Malinowski in an attempt to delimit **context** to a particular situation. Thus, to take one of Malinowski's examples, the context of situation of garden conver- sation relates to a specific location (in the South Seas) where garden talk is so common and repetitive that it conveys no extra **meaning** to the situation and may therefore be regarded as **phatic communion**.

contrastive analysis Makes comparisons between Lx and Ly. Diachronic studies examine the connections over time in the **language** 'family tree', such as the relationships between Latin and French, Italian etc. or between Old English and Middle English. Relationships between Lx and Ly also involve differences; these are important to students of applied linguistics because they illustrate the variety of ways in which human language manifests itself in different ways. Thus analyses of the ways in which unrelated languages operate (for example Hopi and German) are legitimate forms of language comparison. In **language teaching,** contrastive analysis was influential in the heyday of **structuralism**: it was thought to be a necessary prerequisite to the preparation of **teaching materials**, based on the major structural differences between Lx (the learner's L1) and Ly (their **target language**). Such materials and their emphasis on likely learning problems worked most effectively for

phonology and less well, if at all, for other structural systems. This is hardly surprising, given the closed nature of the phonological system. The advent of notions of **communicative competence** appears to have made contrastive analysis less appealing, but it has to be said that contrastive analysis never lived up to the claims made for it. See also **error analysis, language distance.**

conversation The interaction among two or more people, usually face-to-face, but now also by telephone, video and various electronic means. Since email is one form of electronic link, it is interesting to ask if email (or mobile phone 'texting') is a form of conversation, because if it is (agreed that) it is, then the door is open to regard normal written (snailmail) letters also as conversation.

conversation analysis see **CA**

corpus linguistics A collection of spoken or written linguistic data, mostly textual, which can be used for linguistic description or for the verification of hypotheses about a language. Data of these kinds have always been collected: the advent of computers means that now checks and analyses are much faster and probably more accurate. See also **language corpus.**

correctness **Language uses** that are correct are those that conform to the rules of the **code** (**dialect, variety** etc.) of which they form part. Such rules apply to the structures of the code (for example its **grammar**). In order for a form or use to be labelled +/– correct it must have been codified; in other words, it is in **standard languages** that forms are described as being +/– correct. Functional language uses – for example pragmatic (see **pragmatics**), **discourse** – are said to be acceptable or unacceptable rather than correct or incorrect. Correctness more widely concerns the attitude of prescriptivism (see **prescription**) which canvasses against 'bad' English (or other language) and for 'good' English (or other language), by which is meant rule- or **norm**-based use. This attitude is most on display in relation to the written language and tends to be critical of a small set of shibboleths.

Council of Europe A European cultural organisation which has been much involved in the development of **language teaching**. The **functional-notional** syllabus originated in a Council of Europe project to establish a threshold level for the basic linguistic requirements for language learners in different situations, and of course in different languages. More recently, the Council of Europe has built on this threshold level to develop its Common European Framework of References for Languages, Learning, Teaching and Assessment, which is meant to establish a framework of common standards for both teaching and **testing languages**, rather like a common European monetary currency.

courtroom interaction Participants in (legal) courts of law, for example judges, lawyers (advocates, barristers, solicitors), witnesses, defendants and accusers, all have roles to play in trials, and all have customary ways of using **language** to address the court and to interact with its other members. Analysis of these talkings, often by **discourse analysis** or CA, can uncover the rules being employed, the extent to which these are broken (and whether it matters) and how far all **stakeholders** are treated fairly.

creativity The ability to develop something original.

Creative ability has a wide provenance: farmers, scientists, architects and merchants can all express creative ability. But creativity is usually reserved for individual and admired success in the arts. It must be individual (although it could be a group contribution, for example that of the Beatles) and it must be admired. Thus McGonagall's poetry, though individual, never expressed creativity. Literary creativity is associated with **native speaker** (or native speaker-like) control of **language** and as such can support the emergence into **prestige** use of a non-standard dialect (for example Chaucer's decision to write in English).

creoles Mixed codes that achieve a stable state and become the L1 of the rising generation. There is a view that all new languages develop first as unstable **pidgins** which operate as **lingua francas** and then stabilise into creoles with their own **native speakers**. Creoles may not be understood by speakers of the original source language; for example, Haitian Creole is not intelligible to speakers of French, its original source.

criterion An external variable (such as a degree examination) which can be used to judge the validity of a test. What the test attempts to do is to represent the criterion; performance on the test is then used to predict a candidate's performance on the criterion. The term also refers to an acceptable level of knowledge of or performance in a particular domain, or the quality of a response, for example how effective it was. See also **language testing**.

critical applied linguistics A politicised view of **applied linguistics**, which is itself influenced by critical pedagogy, **critical discourse analysis** and, more generally, critical approaches throughout the social sciences and humanities, which may be generally labelled as postmodern (see **postmodernism**), critical of the modernist solutions and their grand narratives. Critical applied linguistics rebukes applied linguistics (the traditional variety) for not being anti-establishment and for not making social change part of its *raison d'être*. Many traditional applied linguists, where they might welcome social change and actively pursue it as individuals, do not regard it as an appropriate criterion of academic research, since it prejudges outcomes. A more telling criticism of critical applied linguistics perhaps is that it refrains from proposing interventions and explanations, which do seem necessary in an applied discipline. What should you teach next week? What should your **test** contain if it is not to embody paternalist and establishment values? On these and all such matters, critical applied linguistics is silent. See also **critical language testing**.

critical discourse analysis A politicised school of **discourse analysis**, which seeks to uncover the underlying **ideology** of the **texts** under analysis. Serious discourse analysts (for example Fairclough) make clear that they bring their own ideology, often Marxist, to the investigation of a text's discourse.

critical language testing An attempt to critique language testing from an ethical point of view, revealing its misuses, in particular the extent to which it supports existing structures of power and fails to contribute to the struggle for emancipation. As such it follows older critical approaches, such as **critical applied linguistics**. See also **critical discourse analysis, ethics, native speaker**.

critical (or **sensitive**) **period** The hypothesis states that there is a stage in normal human development from childhood through puberty to adulthood which is critical or sensitive, meaning that it is at this point (typically associated with the onset of puberty) that, physically and mentally, the child changes into the adult. This is particularly the case for sexual characteristics and, it is argued, also for the **cognitive development** that changes the way in which learning operates. What this means for language learning is that after the critical period it is necessarily SLL, since **first language learning** depends on the learning mechanisms that operate only pre-puberty. On the basis of this hypothesis it is argued that it is not possible to become a **native speaker** of Ly after the critical period.

cross-cultural communication Communication (of information, ideas, feelings etc.) between people from different cultural backgrounds. Such communication can be problematic: the extent to which the problems are linguistic or cultural (or a mixture of both) is much discussed and sometimes researched. In part this explains why the Sapir-Whorf hypothesis of **linguistic relativity** attracts support.

cross-sectional studies A compromise experimental design. Studies of the effect of treatment (such as teaching in education, drugs in medicine) on a sample of subjects requires time, the period during which the treatment interaction may or may not take hold. Pre- and post-**tests** (before and after the intervention) are a necessary part of these studies, which are known as **longitudinal studies**. But often they are not possible for reasons of practicality, finance, personnel etc. Cross-sectional studies offer a compromise. In them there are typically two groups, one not being treated (the 'pre-test' group), the other that has already been treated (the 'post-test' group).

culture Culture has (at least) two important meanings. The first is the anthropological sense, which means a community's behaviours, myths and beliefs which operate unthinkingly. The second sense refers to the dichotomy between the 'high' and the 'low' culture available to members of a community. 'High' culture includes various types of valued art forms. One of the political struggles of the last century has been to develop means of giving value and **prestige** to popular culture. **Language** is both part of a community's culture and also an important means of conveying and acting out its culture.

curriculum Curriculum and **syllabus** are sometimes used interchangeably, but there are two ways in which they are distinguished. In the first, curriculum encompasses the totality of the teaching provision in a school or college or educational system, while syllabus refers to the content of one subject, its grading and **assessment** and sometimes too its **methodology**. In the second, curriculum refers to the range of courses offered in one subject, for example, Applied Linguistics, its content, philosophy, specific purposes and **assessment** criteria, while syllabus refers to the content of one component (in this case, of Applied Linguistics), for example, **SLAR**, listing the topics and the readings for each session.

D

deaf education Children who are non-hearing (deaf) from birth are usually educated in special schools. In more traditional special schools they are taught to speak the local **language** so that they may interact with the hearing community. In order to do so, they must also learn to lip-read. In less traditional schools children are taught (or at least permitted) to use the local **sign language**. (They may also learn to speak and lip-read.) Sign languages are languages that use visual rather than oral signals. Whether or not children are taught to speak the local language, they will certainly interact with one another and with other members of the non-hearing community in the local sign language. What is at issue is whether the school or institution accepts the sign language and uses it as a **medium of instruction**. See also **ASL, BSL**.

decoding All messages, from informal **conversation** to secret intelligence **codes,** need to be decoded (made sense of) by their receivers. For fluent **native speakers** the decoding of informal conversation is automatic and unthinking. Decoding of more complex (and original) messages is time-consuming and may be problematic.

decreolisation Occurs when a **creole** language is increasingly influenced by its source language and becomes more like it, shedding the simplification and admixture that marked its original pidginisation.

deep structure The abstract syntactic representation of a sentence which shows relationship across sentences and clarifies potential ambiguities. In the original theory, the deep structure was said to be linked to the **surface structure** by means of a transformational component. This two-level conceptualisation of grammatical structure has been challenged in recent years.

delexicalisation The process whereby a **language** loses technical terms, prior to relexicalisation, which refers to the stage before new additions are incorporated from contact languages.

descriptive statistics The branch of statistics that reports measures of **variables**, for example mean (average) and standard deviation. To be distinguished from inferential statistics, which describes relationships among variables. Statistics describe samples rather than populations (which are described by parameters), and therefore are dependent for their accuracy on the relationship between the sample and the population of which it forms part.

dialect Distinct use of **grammar** and **vocabulary**, usually marking the geographical origin of its users. Current emphasis on urban rather than rural provenance retains the geographical basis for difference (some cities exhibit group-related difference by locality), but what distinguishes urban from rural dialect studies is the emphasis on **social class** as a dialect marker (taken from Labov). Typically, one dialect is selected as the **prestige** form and designated as the **standard language**. Dialects not selected as the standard language are said to lack an army and a navy because they lack power and privilege. The provision of and expansion of the standard to whole populations is a major contribution of **education**. Standard dialects manifest themselves mainly in **writing**, but education also impacts on the spoken language, such that there is a drift among the educated to use standard (that is, prestige) forms in speech as well as in writing.

dictation A traditional form of **assessment** which is now enjoying a revival. In teaching, dictation is a method for habituating learners of a second language to the stress, intonation and phonemic contrasts of the **target language** and to the need to predict future meanings on the basis of current understanding (the 'reduction of uncertainty' idea). (Dictation has also been used in the teaching of the **mother tongue**, largely to improve and foster **comprehension**.) In **testing,** dictation is used to determine the extent to which learners can (a) operate with **accuracy** the formal conventions and (b) make sense of the **meaning** of the whole **text.** Without the second sense there is little point in mastery of the first.

dictionary A word list giving meanings (monolingual dictionaries) and **translation** from Lx to Ly (bilingual dictionaries). The amount of definitional information provided depends on the cost, size and purpose of the dictionary. The advent of **corpus linguistics** has simplified the data collection necessary for a dictionary. Preparation and publication of a dictionary seem to be necessary first stages on a language's road to **standardisation.**

diglossia As first used by Ferguson, this meant the use in a community of two varieties (see **language varieties**) of one **language** (for example Classical and Egyptian Standard Arabic), each of which has a distinct set of functions, characterised by Ferguson as High (or formal) and Low (or informal). The term has been widened to take account of similar H(igh)–L(ow) distinctions in situations where the two **codes** are unrelated (e.g. Spanish and Guarani in Paraguay), but since formal language typically is different from informal, such broadening of the meaning of diglossia is not helpful.

discourse The term has come to have a range of meanings, from the narrowly linguistic (the verbal record of a **speech event**) to the political, where the interest is in the framework of **knowledge** and **power.** It is the last meaning which is the focus of attention for **critical discourse analysis.** Across this range, discourse and

language change places: where discourse is narrowly interpreted, discourse is part of language; where it is widely interpreted, language becomes part of discourse.

discourse analysis The study of **discourse** (in its first sense) so as to uncover its **structure** and **norms**. Discourse analysis is the study of the **grammar** of discourse.

discourse communities Communities that share **discourses** and distribute **power** unequally, rewarding those who have greater mastery of these discourses, which include conventions, practices, cultures and **language**. Examples of discourse communities are the legal profession, a prison, the army, football fans, a family, women.

distance The extent to which languages share linguistic characteristics. Thus the Germanic languages (English, German etc.) may be said to be less distant from one another than, say, Basque and Castilian Spanish. See also **language distance**.

doctor–patient discourse The professional interaction between a medical doctor and his or her patient, which is characterised by the doctor's attempts both to convey and to control the medical information she or he thinks relevant in non-medical language, and by the patient's, endeavours to access the information about his or her medical condition while lacking the necessary medical knowledge. Medical professionalism requires that the doctor simplifies without trivialising.

domains A domain is the social correlate of a register. Thus the register of drill commands is used in the domain of army training camps, and the register of legalese in the domain of courtroom trials. Domain itself is a usefully

non-theoretical term which can be used to refer to any
context or situation in which a particular **language
variety** is used.

E

EAP English for academic purposes. The limitation and
description of English as used by students, teachers and
researchers in and for higher education. The idea of EAP
became popular with the rapid growth in the latter half
of the twentieth century of numbers of overseas (international) students studying in higher education in
English-speaking countries and needing to acquire
adequate and relevant proficiency in the **language**, but
not needing, so it was claimed, English other than
academic. It is disputed whether (a) academic English
can be divided off in this way and (b) students have no
need (or less need) for the English they encounter outside
the academy. See also **academic discourse**.

Ebonics Another term for African American Vernacular
English (**AAVE**), Ebonics came to prominence over the
decision of the Oakland School Board (in California)
to accord it an official status in the school system. The
Board's decision, which was quickly withdrawn, was
derided by the press and by many African Americans,
but defended on both linguistic and sociolinguistic
grounds by some linguists. It seems that there was never
any question of recognition being given to a written
Ebonics; the Board was attempting to recognise (and
support) actual practice in Oakland classrooms, where
spoken interaction is a mix of Ebonics and Standard
American English.

ECAL *Edinburgh Course in Applied Linguistics*. A four-volume publication (Oxford University Press, 1973–7) in which the Edinburgh University Department of Applied Linguistics laid out its **teaching materials,** its key reading texts and its theoretical discussions of **applied linguistics,** which had informed the first ten years of its own postgraduate teaching. The Edinburgh department was the first named university department of applied linguistics and these four volumes were for a time influential.

Edinburgh Course in Applied Linguistics see **ECAL**

ecology of language A descriptive approach to the variety (see **language varieties**) of **language use** in a given situation, a term with its origin in both botany and anthropology.

education The provision of teaching by institutional means through schools, colleges etc. The **language learning** that takes place in educational institutions is necessarily group-related and needs to be distinguished from the kind of learning enjoyed on their own by individuals, often referred to as **acquisition** in relation to language.

educational linguistics In an attempt to provide a more coherent definition of **applied linguistics,** Spolsky offered this term as a means of limiting the area of interest. 'Educational linguistics' is certainly narrower but since many, perhaps most, applied linguists are involved in some aspect of language teaching, that may be no bad thing. The term, however, appears not to have been widely taken up.

EFL English as a foreign language. In many non-English speaking countries, English has for many years been taught as a foreign language. But the acronym EFL refers particularly to the explosion of interest in the UK and later in Ireland, the USA, Canada, Australia and New Zealand in teaching their English (as a foreign language) throughout the world. The increasing demand has been important commercially to the UK and these other countries for the provision of teachers and materials for the teaching of English as a foreign language (TEFL) and in the recruitment of EFL students to attend courses in higher education (including English language schools) in the anglophone countries. This is now a major educational industry. In addition, EFL has been important as a major source for and target of **applied linguistics** courses and as a driving influence, no doubt in part because it has attracted considerable financial support, on the **assessment** of **language assessment** generally and on the broader teaching of modern languages in the UK and elsewhere. See also **LOTE**.

elaborated code The term used by Bernstein to indicate one of the varieties of language used to convey meaning in a social **context**. Bernstein claimed that those using the elaborated code would make a greater use of adjectives, use a more complicated sentence structure and the pronoun 'I', while those accustomed to the **restricted code** would have a more restricted **vocabulary** range, use more question tags and the pronouns 'he' and 'she' in place of nouns. What those employing the elaborated code were capable of was removing themselves from their accounts, and writing (and speaking) generally rather than with reference to their own specific experience Although Bernstein was not specifically addressing the issue of language, since he was equally interested in context and social role, his work was widely interpreted unfavourably as comparing the working class (restricted code users) and the middle class (elaborated code users). Earlier names for the restricted and elaborated polarities were private and public.

elicitation techniques Methods developed by phoneticians and linguists to describe the phonological and grammatical systems of a **language variety**. Native speaker informants are used by the investigators to produce a **phonology** and a **grammar**. Such products are of course metalinguistic and do not guarantee that the linguist or phonetician have themselves become speakers of the language. See also **metalanguage**.

EliF English as a lingua franca. A concept related to **English as an international language**, the idea of EliF is based on a corpus of EFL uses. The rationale is that most English use in the world today is between **non-native speakers** and that what they are using is EliF. This needs to be described and promoted. Like English as an international language, it represents an attack on the **native speaker** and suffers just as much from the consequent loss of a definable model.

-emic approach The linguistic description of the phonology or phonemics of a language variety which determines whether the sound system of the variety is distinct. Differences among speakers there may be, but these are ignored for the purpose of the group description. Individual differences are accounted for in an **-etic** (or **phonetic**) description.

encyclopedias The encyclopedists in France, and later the computers of the UK's *Encyclopaedia Britannica*, attempted to encompass all human knowledge in their volumes. Modern encyclopedias are less ambitious, seeking to cover one area such as **linguistics** or **applied linguistics**. The relation between encyclopedias (with their accounts), **dictionaries** (with their definitions) and the hybrid encyclopedic dictionaries is of interest.

endangered languages Minority **languages** which are in decline and facing **language death**. The sentimental view is that of Dr Johnson: 'I am always sorry when any language is lost, because languages are the pedigree of nations'; and that the loss of a language is similar to the loss of a botanical or zoological species. As such it diminishes the world's variety (see **language varieties**). But there is another view, that language death has always occurred and that new languages have, so far, emerged to take their place. Languages are endangered not because they are dying but because their speakers are: the canonical example is that of a small remote community where there are few inhabitants, all old. Undoubtedly languages become endangered through contact with languages of wider impact such as English or Arabic, but they are also at risk (exacerbated no doubt by their contact with a global language) from their lack of modernising power and reach, so that they lose appeal and become unattractive to the young. Many pressure and scholarly groups exist to promote and maintain endangered languages, but there is a strong argument that when a language becomes endangered and attracts maintenance support, it is already too late to revive it. See also **hybridity, language maintenance**.

English as a foreign language see EFL

English as a lingua franca see EliF

English as a second language see ESL

English as an international language (also referred to as **International English**) The attempt to develop and promote a common **language** which is not based on the **native speaker** model of **British English, American English** etc. The problem with developing and implementing such a **code** is that it is not clear which model it depends on. This assumes, of course, that all **language learning** is model-based, and ultimately that the model in question is that of an educated native speaker. An alternative view of English as an international language is that it means everyone's English in intercultural use; that is, that I use my English to speak to, say, a Japanese academic, who uses his or her English to speak to me.

English for academic purposes see **EAP**

English for speakers of other languages see **ESOL**

English for specific purposes see **ESP**

error The occurrence in speaking or in writing of a language item which does not conform to the rules of the language, or, in other words, is regarded by an educated **native speaker** as ungrammatical or inappropriate. See also **error analysis**.

error analysis The natural applied concomitant to the descriptive **contrastive analysis**, this is the investigation of **target language** errors made by learners with a view to their amelioration and the provision of remedial **teaching materials**. While mistakes were seen as random and individual, errors were regarded as group-related and therefore based traditionally on the contrast between the learner's L1 and the target language. Corder's realisation that errors were indicative of learning progress and therefore of **interlanguage** paved the way for the development of **SLAR**.

ESL English as a second language. The term has been used synonymously with **EFL**, but more helpfully its distinct use is for situations in which English is not the L1 but the **medium of instruction** and/or widely used in the local **context**. Thus Japan is an EFL situation while Zambia is an ESL situation. It is unclear whether those from an EFL situation (e.g. Japanese) who come to an English language school thereby become ESL students. Attempting such precision is probably a trivial pursuit.

ESOL English for speakers of other languages. A useful cover term that comprehends **EFL** and **ESL** and at the same time recognises in a now somewhat patronising way that there are languages other than English. The reverse term is used in Australia – Languages other than English (**LOTE**) – to refer to the teaching of modern languages.

ESP English for specific purposes. Like **EAP**, this attempts to delimit the extent of English needed for study and training on the basis of subject area; thus English for science, English for medicine, English for oil-drilling. ESP has received large teaching and **testing** development but, attractive though it is, especially to those who themselves **research** and teach subject areas, it remains problematic. Theoretically there is no clear basis for language division, and in practice one specific purpose overlaps with another, and within specific purposes themselves there are further specific purposes, like Chinese boxes: for example the English of medicine (the English of surgery (the English of paediatric surgery)).

Esperanto The most successful of a group of **artificial languages** developed in Europe in the late nineteenth century. The aim in all cases was to foster international understanding. Esperanto remains active today but suffers not just from the lack of **native speakers** but also from its narrow linguistic base, mainly in the Romance languages.

essay An extended piece of writing, more formal than the **composition**. Often set as an exercise, it requires students to express a **point of view** on a given topic or explore an argument.

ethical code A public written statement by an organisation of its principled approach to its professional and/or business activities.

ethics The advent of postmodern challenges, the critique of **critical applied linguistics,** and the widespread embrace of professionalism have encouraged a greater awareness of the demands of ethics and a concern to make that awareness explicit. This has led to discussion, conferences and publications on ethics in **applied linguistics** and its component parts, and to declarations of the **ethical codes** to which applied linguists subscribe. Whether such efforts have contributed to more ethical behaviour by applied linguists is unclear. 'Ethics' and 'morality' are often used interchangeably, although sometimes 'ethics' is more clearly associated with public issues and 'morality' with private ones; thus 'morality' relates to individual conscience and 'ethics' to public and professional conduct. The professionalising of applied linguistics, like that of other endeavours, has led to an interest in determining (and declaring) just what is the ethical basis of those who regard themselves as applied linguists. It does seem to be the case that to be professional means to take an ethical stance, but while applied linguistics resembles other professions (long training, public mission) it lacks the sanction of expulsion that the older professions (medicine, the law) enjoy. See also **profession**.

ethnic identity The various genetic and social features that make up an individual's **identity**. See **ethnicity**.

ethnicity That bundle of characteristics that provide an individual with his or her **identity**. The term is normally confined to acquired characteristics (language, religion, historical affinity), but some commentators extend its meaning to include also genetic characteristics (race, age, gender). According to Barth, ethnicity is defined not by its content but by its boundaries. Thus membership is prior to what it stands for.

ethnography The classical anthropological method of **research**, involving close observation (often participant observation) and subsequently a written report. In **applied linguistics** the term refers to an important area of research and to reflection on **language use**. See also **ethnography of communication, ethnography of speaking, qualitative research**.

ethnography of communication The study of methods and systems of **communication** in a given community or situation, including **language**, sign systems, cultural markers etc.

ethnography of speaking A mnemonic offered by Hymes for the ethnography of speaking (or of **communication**), offering an -**etic** framework of **speech event** components, the argument being that all are present in every speech event. The components are: setting a scene; participants; ends (purposes, outcomes); act sequences (message form and content); key (attitudinal aspects); instrumentalities (norms and styles of speech); norms of interaction and interpretation; and genre (the discourse type). Members of communities have an inbuilt **competence** in operating these components appropriately (just as they have a linguistic competence). It is the speaking competence that underlies the concept of **communicative competence.**

ethnomethodology The sociological adjunct to phenomenology, ethnomethodology is the study of common-sense behaviours. Its **language** interest has been in the assumptions speakers make in their everyday interactions with one another and is therefore related to **CA**. Garfinkel's breaching experiments are a notable example of the taking-for-grantedness of much normal human interaction.

-etic approach The phonetic correlate of the phonemic **-emic approach**. -Etic analyses are far more detailed and therefore suitable for individual descriptions, but it should be noted that two quite distinct -etic descriptions (of two individuals) can be reconciled into a single -emic description.

exceptional learner It is generally accepted that second language learners who begin acquisition of the second language after the **critical period** do not become native speakers. However, there is evidence that some (probably a small number) of such learners do gain the same skills and knowledge that **native speakers** have: these are the so-called exceptional learners. But it should be noted that some researchers claim that cognitively there is still a difference.

F

face In interaction, participants need to give positive impressions of themselves. Maintaining face, or not losing face, is important for self-esteem and to enable others to respect one's participation in the interaction. Societies differ markedly in the ways in which face is both preserved and lost.

feedback In **conversation**, confirmation by the interlocutor that the speaker is understood. Such confirmation is typically empty of meaning (phatic) consisting of grunts, space-fillers (e.g. 'mm'). In **discourse analysis**, these are referred to as back-channel cues (see **back-channel responses**). See also **phatic communion.**

feminist linguistics There are several strands to this topic. They include the investigation of: (a) **gender** differences in **language**, which range from marked sex distinctions (he/she) to grammatical declension (masculine, feminine, neuter); (b) the treatment of females as inferior or even invisible (the use of male deictics to refer to both males and females), which may be more problematic and obvious in languages which, unlike English, are heavily marked for grammatical gender; and (c) the linguistic markers of social disapproval of all female expression and appearance (the unbalanced ratio of condemnatory terms for females, e.g. bitch, slag, vis-à-vis equivalent negative terms for males is well documented).

field-specific tests see **LSP, ESP**

first language The language to which the child is first exposed and of which she or he becomes a **native speaker**. Related terms are **mother tongue**, which seems to be equivalent to first language, and 'dominant language' and 'home language', both of which have somewhat different senses.

first language acquisition The study of language acquisition by the child. Data from the large number of such studies, covering many languages, demonstrate a consistent pattern of staged progress. It is argued that first language acquisition is not replicable and that without it in Lx there is no possibility of becoming a **native speaker** in Ly. At the same time **SLAR** continues to debate whether the acquisition of a second language repeats first language acquisition processes (and stages) or whether it operates a quite different – and unique – programme.

first language education This is used in two ways:
(a) Education at school (primary and secondary) in the medium of the first or home language. It should be noted that for large numbers of children, perhaps the majority world-wide, this is not possible, largely for practical reasons (few teachers able to use the language, no teaching materials and, in the extreme case, no written code). The **BICS** position is that children do not progress cognitively without first language provision. This, it is argued, is necessary for later **CALP** to become possible.
(b) Education about the first language. This, in its strict linguistic aspect, is now less common than it used to be, and as far as English is concerned it is uncommon today to find schools teaching their students the **grammar** of English. But there certainly are other aspects of teaching about the language, especially its discourse and its cultures, in lessons on composition, on history, **culture**,

literature etc. See also **medium of instruction.**

fluency Often used in contrast to **accuracy.** While accuracy relates to linguistic forms, fluency seems more concerned with language **functions.** Fluency therefore has to do with the **ability** to maintain an interaction and where appropriate to speak (or write meaningfully) on a given topic for longer than a few seconds. It should be noted that fluency is a primitive (non-theoretical) term, in the sense that it has no theoretical basis and no generally accepted definition among applied linguists.

focus on form Incidental teaching of **grammar** issues as they happen to arise in the course of teaching is referred to as focus on form. This is distinguished from **focus on forms.**

focus on forms The deliberate and explicit teaching of grammar. Often known as consciousness raising, this is distinguished from **focus on form.**

folk linguistics Knowledge and beliefs about language held by people in general, for example views about **correctness.** Also the study of these beliefs by linguists.

foregrounding A stylistic device which brings into prominence a word (or idea) that normal or unmarked syntax would not emphasise.

foreign language Any language which is not the speaker's **mother tongue** or **first language** or of which he or she is not **a native speaker.** In **language teaching** and in **sociolinguistics,** 'foreign language' tends to be used of a speech situation in which the language of instruction (the **target language**) is in use only or largely in class.

This is distinct from the second language situation, where the second language is one of those commonly used informally in the community and often the medium of school instruction. See also **ESL**.

foreigner talk Stereotyped language of **non-native speaker;** the simplified speech used by **native speakers** to address non-native speakers. It is slower, louder, has simplified **syntax** and morphology and exaggerates content words. It is unclear whether foreigners themselves ever talk like this. See also **simplification**.

forensic linguistics The use of linguistic and particularly phonetic techniques to investigate taped police interviews with suspected criminals, as well as the transcripts of the criminals' written and spoken testimony and the police records of their interviews. Such analyses enable decisions to be made on authorship of the transcripts and on whether the records have been later doctored. As with forensic science more broadly, the work in forensic linguistics largely seeks to answer the question: to whom does this X (body, body part, spoken or written data) belong?

form Form in language refers to the structural features used in speech and **writing,** as compared with the function(s) for which those features are being used.

fossilisation A state of **language learning** which is incomplete or partial but which is not changing or improving. What this suggests is that the learner is somehow satisfied with the stage reached, finding it adequate for his or her purposes. Adult migrants often achieve fossilised states, living as they do in a bilingual situation where their L1 is used for many personal and social functions and the L2 (the fossilised **code**) only for specific public purposes. A fossilised state is steady: just as there is unlikely to be progress, so there is unlikely to be **back-sliding** and **language loss**. In other words the learner has achieved a viable **interlanguage**. (Although the L2 is generally regarded as representing the fossilised state, there is a sense in which those who have spent many years away from their L1 speech community – aged migrants who arrived in the new country as young adults – may also find their L1 to be fossilised, since it is likely to become fixed at the time of their migration. This is particularly true of those older migrants who have never returned 'home' and who have had no or little input to make up for the changes their L1 has undergone in their 'home' speech community.) See also **SLAR**.

frequency Commonly used of the incidence of **vocabulary** tokens (individual word occurrences), the purpose being to provide differential lists showing those tokens or items that are most frequent in various kinds of written or spoken discourse: the first 1,000, the second 1,000 etc. Such lists are then available for **teaching materials** and **language tests,** the assumption being that what is more frequent is also easier. This is an assumption that needs to be challenged, given that the more frequent items or tokens tend to be short and often vague and ambiguous, for example 'get' or 'may'.

function If function is how **language** is used, its purpose, **form** is how the function is expressed. Thus the dis-tinction made between 'one' and 'many' is a language function, expressed in the form of singular and plural. The distinction male–female is a functional distinction expressed in the gendered forms of masculine and feminine. Language functions are regarded as being categories of behaviour; thus requests, apologies and complaints are functions. Speech functions (or **speech acts**) consist of both literal meaning ('It's cold in here', which is a statement about the room temperature) and understood **meaning** ('I'd like you to close the window', 'bring a shawl', 'turn up the heating' etc.). Different functions can have the same form in English: final -s can stand for the third person singular and mark plurality. Commands can be realised both as imperatives and as declaratives: 'Close the window', 'Shut the door' (imperative); 'You must close the window', 'You will shut the door' (declarative).

functional-notional approach (also **notional-functional,** or **notional,** usually referring to the design of a **syllabus** for **language teaching**). Content is arranged according to necessary meanings and functions required by the learner and available in the language. They are presented in some order of likely or assumed frequency. Functional-notional approaches are based in some sense on the model of notional **grammar,** which assumes that functional categories such as tense, **gender** and number are universally available but differentially distributed. Notional grammars are at bottom versions of traditional grammars. See also **curriculum.**

G

gender Gender in language has two senses:
(a) The linguistic correlate of the sexual distinction. Thus in English males and females are indicated by 'he' and 'she'.
(b) A variant method of grammatical categorisation whereby groups of nouns are distinguished from one another in terms of their case endings (or other

morphological features) and agreement rules. There is no close isomorphism between sex and gender in this grammatical categorisation. Nouns appear to be assigned quite randomly to one or other gender except those referring to humans, although even there anomalies appear: thus *Das Madchen* uses a neuter article to indicate a female subject. It seems likely that this second use of gender was once dominant and that as it disappeared largely in languages such as English (compared with languages such as Latin) the prevalence of human sex differences became more prominent and more open to critique.

generalisability theory An extension of classical test theory, differing largely in its view of measurement error. Classical test theory considers **error** to be a single entity, while generalisability theory estimates the contribution to error of its various sources, employing the statistical package known as the analysis of variance (ANOVA) technique.

genre Traditionally, genre is regarded as a class of speech events; thus the genre of academic articles, the genre of love poetry, the genre of political speeches. It is not always distinguished from **register,** although register is more helpfully understood as describing the style or variety (see **language varieties**) of a particular group or profession; thus the register of lawyers, the register of racing car enthusiasts. More recent discussions of genre have been influenced by **critical discourse analysis** and are more ethnographic, associating genre with a **discourse community** and with socially ratified ways of using language in connection with a social activity, thereby empowering some members of society, oppressing others. See also **academic discourse, ESP.**

genre analysis Different approaches to **genre** include: (a) the system functional approach, involving studies of encounters and reports based on **systemic functional linguistics**; (b) the **ESP** approach, which offers a set of functionally defined stages, moves and steps and associates genres with particular **discourse communities**; (c) the new rhetoric approach, less linguistic, offering an ethnographic-type analysis, examining the wide views and beliefs of the communities of use; and (d) the **critical discourse analysis** approach, which distinguishes **style**, **discourse** and genre, probing for the ways in which genre is indicative of the unequally distributed symbolic capital of society.

grammar Concerns the rules for word (and phrase) formation and for their combination in sentences. These two types of structure are termed morphology and **syntax**. At its simplest, grammar can be thought of as the skeleton of a **language**, while the way sentences are used in **discourse** and text is its flesh. Grammar is also said to indicate the speaker's **knowledge** of the language and, even more abstractly, the language capacity that all humans have. Metaphorically, grammar provides a model for any rule-based social system (the grammar of music, the grammar of advertising).

grammar translation method The traditional method of **language teaching**, involving the explicit teaching of the grammar and employing translation between Lx and Ly (both ways) as the main teaching exercise. This method is still in use, though less so since the mid-twentieth century. The method was devised (or developed) for the teaching of Latin and Greek. The object was to instil intellectual rigour and transmit the cultural values embodied in the classical literary canon. It succeeded, where it did, because it was not concerned with the spoken language, because it dealt with a limited **corpus** (both languages were dead) and because the teaching went on over a very long time span. Its transfer to the teaching of modern foreign languages was always problematic and set up a tension between language teaching as an academic discipline, **knowledge** based, and language teaching as communicative, integrative activity, a tension which is still very much alive today.

grammaticality judgements Tests designed to distinguish educated native speakers from educated and highly proficient **non-native speakers**. Such tests have been shown to be more sensitive than other measures or types of analysis in marking the distinction between **native speakers** and non-native speakers. It is important in such studies that the two groups are matched in every way except, of course, in terms of childhood acquisition. See also **childhood language acquisition, SLAR.**

grapheme The smallest unit of a **writing system** capable of causing a contrast in meaning. In English the 26 units of the alphabet are the main graphemes. See also **phoneme.**

H

hegemony The concept introduced by the Italian Marxist Antonio Gramsci which holds that political control is exerted through the operation of an invisible power structure. It takes for granted the co-opting of the working classes into the bourgeoisie, rendering them subservient to and complicit in the ruling class's **ideology**. An example that has been proposed is the use of **Standard English** as a typical focus of such indoctrination – although on reflection the acquisition of

Standard English, so far as it went, acted more in the interests of the working classes than of the ruling class.

heteroglossia The notion, formulated by Voloshinov and Bahktin, that **language** is inherently dialogic rather than monologic and that there is no such thing as a unitary language, since all language use co-exists with a multiplicity of different ways of speaking that are constantly intermingling with each other. See also **language variety**.

heteronymy This refers to a **language variety** that has not been standardised and is dependent on a corresponding autonomous standard. The varieties of English spoken in the Caribbean are in a heteronymous relation to **Standard English**, in which all official communication, including literary creation, takes place.

hybridity The view that language and cultures are and always have been resilient to intermingling: an argument that has been used to combat the claims of **linguistic imperialism**.

hypercorrection Accommodation to a **norm** that goes too far because of anxiety about possible failure. The resultant accommodation is therefore inappropriate. In my own case, a South Wales upbringing and a desire to accommodate towards **RP** caused me to change my open vowels to diphthongs, thus: boat (/but/)→/bəut/; but anxiety leads to the inappropriate use of dipthongs, thus: fort (/fut/)→/fəut/, and coat (/cut/)→/cəut/.

hypothesis A conjecture about language use which is stated so as to allow for its own falsification; for example, 'Students who study French for five hours a day for four weeks will perform better at the end of the semester than students who study for one hour a day for sixteen weeks.' Such a statement is testable and therefore open to falsification. Hypotheses are common in **quantitative research,** which begins with a set of **research** questions. The hypotheses are sometimes stated, typically in the null form (for example, 'There is no difference between the control and the experimental group'); more often they are implicit in the research questions. Statistical analyses are designed to test formally the probabilities that the hypotheses are true (more correctly, that they cannot be rejected) and typically include some kind of probability statement which indicates that there is less than a 1 per cent (or, more generously, 5 per cent) probability that the observed difference or relationship has occurred by chance, or in other words that it is random.

I

IAAL International Association of Applied Linguistics. See **AILA.**

IATEFL International Association of Teachers of English as a Foreign Language, begun in the 1960s in the UK with the deliberate intention of making its international basis as distinct from the American **TESOL** organisation as possible. Since its beginnings, IATEFL has attracted foreign (that is, non-UK-based) members, but it is not clear how far its reach has extended internationally or how far it has loosed the UK's hegemonic grip. A similar criticism could be made (and is) of TESOL. IATEFL exists to provide a professional backing to all teachers of **EFL** through conferences and seminars, newsletters and a journal: the *English Language Teaching Journal* is sponsored by IATEFL.

identity The sense of selfhood, achieved for most people through belonging, or wishing to belong, to various ethnic groups, some of which are ascribed, some attained. Language is clearly a powerful symbol since its use is constantly reinforced through interaction. Learning a second language, and wishing to do it well, can create a problem of identity if the learner comes to feel that by choosing to pass in Ly she or he is rejecting his or her identity in Lx.

ideographic A system of written script in which each character (or ideogram) has an abstract or conventional meaning, not linked to external reality. Chinese graphemes are commonly referred to as ideograms although they are word-based rather than concept- or thing-based. It is therefore more appropriate (though not common) to refer to Chinese writing as logographic.

ideologies 'Ideology' is used in two main senses. The first is that of false consciousness or a set of misapprehensions regarding reality. The second is more neutral and refers to any system of ideas. The senses are related, but the first is typically used disparagingly. Critical approaches assume that all **texts** are permeated by ideological connotations/**meanings**, which are not immediately obvious except to the trained critical analyst. The purpose, therefore, is to uncover those ideological forces that help maintain the text's structural configurations, and at the same time to contribute to correcting the social injustice which the uncovered ideologies perpetuate. The role of ideology is central to all critical approaches such as **critical applied linguistics**. It is, however, important to remember that just as the text is ideological so too is the analyst. Fairclough's honest and helpful introduction of himself as a Marxist is unusually refreshing.

idiolect The individual **language** of everyone; what it is that one is a **native speaker** of. It is an individual's idiolect that makes recognition (by old friends, family etc.) possible. Neutralising of individual idiolects towards the **standard language** is normally achieved through **education**. Complete neutralisation does not happen, which explains why even highly educated native speakers still disagree with one another on **grammaticality judgements**.

IELTS International English Language Testing System, operated since the late 1980s by three partners: the British Council, the International Development Programme (Australia) and the University of Cambridge Local Examinations Syndicate (UCLES: ESOL). IELTS is the successor to the former British Council **test**, the English Language Testing Service; this itself was a successor to the British Council's earlier **test**, the English Proficiency Test Battery. All three tests were developed in the first instance to determine whether those coming to study in UK (and later Australian) higher **education** had adequate English for that purpose. More recently the range of IELTS has extended to cover several professional organisations (for example, in the UK, medical doctors and nurses) and migrants entering Australia and New Zealand. IELTS exists at present in two versions: general academic and general training. They share two modules (speaking and listening) and have separate reading and writing modules. IELTS is developed and administered by UCLES and is now offered at centres world-wide on fixed dates throughout the year. See also **ability, academic discourse, proficiency, TOEFL**.

ILTA International Language Testing Association, established in 1999 to promote good practice in **language testing**. It sponsors the journal *Language Testing* and an annual conference (in conjunction with the Language Testing Research Colloquium – LTRC), provides financial support for workshops in language testing, and awards annual prizes for the best journal article, MA and PhD theses. Its web page provides information about ILTA, its current officers, its **code of ethics** (see **ethical code**) and current language testing activities.

imagined communities This is a metaphoric explanation by Benedict Anderson of what we mean by a nation (and, *mutatis mutandis*, a **language**). Most of us, he points out, live in societies the vast majority of whose members we never encounter. How is it then that we regard one another as belonging together in a nation? It is, he proposes, because we belong to an imagined community, the **norms** and practices of which we assume as corresponding, however partially, to our own. It is helpful to relate Anderson's view to Brass's discussion of the pool of symbols that define nations, symbols such as race, religion, language and history, a single one of which may be sufficient to foster a unique sense of nationhood. See also **nation and language**.

immersion Immersion programmes were developed first in Montreal by Lambert and colleagues in response to the Canadian government's decision to establish Canada as a bilingual state. In Quebec this was a particular challenge to the many anglophone parents who spoke little or no French themselves and whose children attended English-medium schools. What immersion programmes offered was a full French-medium curriculum for non-francophone children. They were effective, and many anglophone children have progressed through these programmes to near native **fluency** in French with no loss of their English fluency. Such programmes have extended widely across Canada and elsewhere and have spawned a variety of alternatives, including semi-immersion. There are drawbacks: though successful speakers of French, immersion graduates are not **native speakers** and do not control French grammar implicitly as do francophone students. This may be – it is not clear – because for political and/or religious reasons they are separated at school from francophone children and so lack peer interaction in French. It should also be remembered that Canadian immersion is not new: colonial governments have typically provided **education** for local children in the colonists' language. What is different in the Canadian model is that it is voluntary and that there is some doubt as to whether the **target language** is or is not the prestige language. See also **bilingual education, colonial discourse.**

impact The effect of a **test** on individuals, on educational systems and more generally on society; in other words, its effect on all possible stakeholders. See also **washback.**

implicational scaling A statistical technique which assumes that success at any level implies success at all lower levels. The aim is to demonstrate a universal order of second language acquisition. The technique suffers somewhat from the claim that it is unidimensional, thereby failing to take into account all the other **variables** involved in language **performance.** See also **scales, SLAR.**

indigenous African languages Languages that are native to Africa, therefore excluding settler and colonial languages such as French, English and Portuguese. What is truly indigenous is of course always somewhat problematic, since what we now regard as African languages were themselves imports at some point in history. 'Oldest inhabitants' might be a more descriptive term.

individual differences Just as sociology studies groups and their similarities (and their differences from other groups) so psychology studies individuals and their differences. **Testing** is predicated on the fundamental premise that individuals differ both physically and mentally and that the purpose of tests is to measure and describe those differences. The concept of individual difference is also used in **SLAR** to investigate differential achievement in **language learning**. Three sets of explanatory factors have been proposed: social, cognitive and affective; but the field still awaits a comprehensive theory to account for individual differences in language learning. See also **grammaticality judgements**.

informant A linguistic or phonetic informant is (usually) a **native speaker** of the **language** (or the **lect**) that the researcher is investigating. Traditionally it was by questioning the informant that fieldwork was done, both in **linguistics** and in anthropology, but nowadays technology has provided alternatives to face-to-face interviews. See also **language corpus**.

Initial Teaching Alphabet see **ita**

input For **child language acquisition** to take place without problems, two factors are needed. First, the child must himself or herself progress normally through the developmental stages. Second, the **context** must provide adequate **language** activity, both interactive directly with the child and taking place among others in the situation but available for the child to hear. This is input. Without it, however intelligent the child, it will remain speechless. Note that those providing the input need not be the child's parents or other family members. Most often they will be, but any care-givers can provide the necessary input. This does not end when the child goes to school. Once there (even earlier) the child's peers (and teachers) provide further and more varied input, as do contemporary electronic media in many of the more affluent countries. It does not end when adulthood begins, since we all continue to acquire language, in particular new vocabulary. As far as second language acquisition is concerned, input is just as necessary and much more difficult to provide, especially in the typical foreign language classroom. No doubt this is a major reason for the slow and unsuccessful progress of much **second language teaching.** See also **output.**

institutional language The **language** used by members of organisations when at work. That suggests that institutional language is part-way between private and public **language use.** One of the aims of **language planning** is to support institutional language in the workplace rather than to bring about a complete switch in language use.

intelligibility The ease with which a sample of spoken language may be understood. It is influenced by a variety of factors including **accent, intonation,** speed of delivery, the location and duration of pauses, and the listener's ability to predict elements of the speaker's message.

interaction If the purpose of **language** is basically **communication,** then all language events involve interaction. This must be largely true since language is typically dialogic rather than monologic – with the exceptions of diaries, talking to oneself and madness. Even in **writing**, which seems solitary, the writer does have an audience in mind. And yet there is a reluctance to let go altogether of individual autonomy since language is also used, one assumes, for thinking. Reductively this could be termed interacting with oneself. But that makes a mockery of the two-person exchanges which occupy much of our waking life. **Social constructivism**, following Vygotsky and Bahktin, makes interaction primary to all language analysis and applications, including teaching and **assessment**. Less radically, **sociolinguistics** has made its concern with interaction central to its engagement with **communicative competence**, with the view that language is constitutive of social relationships.

interlanguage Learning is a matter of successive attempts at making the right choices and discarding the wrong ones. In SLL, William Nemser called this progression 'proximate systems' while Corder, following Selinker, popularised the term 'interlanguage'. Interlanguage is a dynamic rather than a steady state and is therefore not fossilised, although if it ceases to develop it may become so. Much of **SLAR** is concerned with elaborating the extent to which interlanguage development is rule-based. See also **fossilisation**.

International Association of Applied Linguistics see **AILA**

International Association of Teachers of English as a Foreign Language see **IATEFL**

International English see **English as an international language**

International English Language Testing System see IELTS

International Language Testing Association see ILTA

intonation The systematic use of pitch and rhythm to convey information additional to that expressed by the words themselves.

IRT item response theory. A theory much used in current educational measurement (including **language testing**) which provides a methodology that takes into account both candidate ability and **test item** characteristics.

ita Initial Teaching Alphabet, a project funded by the Pitman Foundation in the 1970s, itself using a specific bequest from the estate of George Bernard Shaw, to develop a new alphabet for English. The purpose was to shorten the amount of time needed in early schooling for children to learn to read with ease. Shaw, who himself experimented with so-called improved spelling, held the view that a written alphabet that approximated more closely to the sounds of the spoken language would achieve that goal. The ita was developed to that end. It consisted of 42 letters: 24 standard lower-case Roman letters and a number of special ones which are modified Roman letters. Each letter represents a single phoneme. **Teaching materials** were developed and a number of schools recruited to participate in the project in the UK and Canada. The evaluation of the project was positive. Test results indicated that children did indeed learn to read more quickly. There were, however, two problems with the project. The first was that while the specially developed ita materials were plentiful, well designed and attractive, the comparison groups using the traditional orthography (t-o) materials were stuck with their old, well-used materials. And so success for the ita schools could be regarded as a halo effect. The second problem was that when the ita children had completed their reading **syllabus** they found transferring to the t-o of the normal books and papers difficult. Indeed, by the time they had finally made the transfer they were back level-pegging with the control t-o children, who had taken the usual length of time to learn to read but of course in doing so had already mastered traditional **orthography**. Ita is little heard of today and is likely to remain a footnote until some dictator decides that all the existing books in English should be transferred to ita. That seems unlikely to happen. See also **curriculum**.

J

jargon 'Jargon' has two meanings:

(a) Speech or **writing** used by a group of people who belong to a particular trade or **profession**. The term is typically disparaging and is used in that way by outsiders: 'they speak jargon' (i.e. we don't). Jargon is perhaps more obvious on the surface than is **register** and may therefore be regarded as the folk view of register, details and features of which require expert analysis, while jargon refers only to certain **vocabulary** items.

(b) A **form** of language which has resulted through pidginisation but is not yet stable; sometimes referred to as a pre-pidgin variety. See also **language variety, pidgin**.

K

kinship terminology The way different cultures express their own particular views of human relationships linguistically offers insights into those cultures and at the same time helps us reflect on how far the linguistic realisations of what are often very different perceptions of relationships are to be viewed as language differences or as cultural (only) differences. The makes possible an awareness of and provides a handle on the fundamental language–culture **interaction. See culture.**

knowledge In **applied linguistics** two uses of this term are particularly relevant: (a) the knowledge that distinguishes a successful learner from a less successful learner; and (b) knowledge as an associate of **power,** thereby signifying power and at the same time excluding those without that knowledge: 'there is no power relation without the correlative constitution of a field of knowledge' (Foucault).

L

language The main human **communication** system, acquired by human infants as part of their normal development. Language is a linguistic entity but also a cultural, social and historical one. It is said by some to keep people apart, whereas for Saussure it is what binds people together. Both views have merit.

language acquisition A broad approach to **child language acquisition,** encompassing both first and second languages. Clearly, in all such cases what is being acquired is (a) language, but, while the distinction between first and subsequent languages acquired is important, it remains unclear to what extent this distinction makes the processes of first and second language acquisition unlike one another. See also **critical period, first language acquisition, language learning, SLL, SLAR.**

language and the law More perhaps than any other professional activity, the law is a **language** issue. Law is written (or otherwise conveyed) in language, its understanding and interpretation depend on analyses and readings, and its determinations are recorded in language. It is not surprising therefore that changing the language which acts as the **medium** of the law is difficult and slow. Changing the language may mean changing all the interpretations and may mean changing the law itself. In most anglophone ex-colonial countries English remains the language of the higher courts and the written repository of the law. See also **ESP, medium of instruction, profession.**

language aptitude The extent to which an individual possesses specific **language learning** ability. **Research** is unclear on the existence of a language aptitude **variable;** various aptitude tests have attempted to define and operationalise the **construct.** The best-known tests are still the Carroll and Sapon Modern Language Aptitude Test and the Language Aptitude Battery. Language aptitude tests normally claim to predict success only in terms of defined learning outcomes or distinct methodologies. Various abilities are reckoned to contribute to language aptitude, abilities such as phonetic coding, grammatical sensitivity, rote learning ability and inductive learning ability. Also thought to be relevant are the ability to make sense of decontextualised data and experience of SLL in early childhood. See also **ability, aptitude, context, methodology.**

language attitude An attitude is a characteristic tendency to react consistently favourably or unfavourably to a stimulus. The stimulus may be a person, an object or a concept. Attitudes tend to be quite stable and less subject to factual input than are beliefs or opinions. In **applied linguistics** the stimulus is a language or speakers of a **language**. To what extent **informants** distinguish between the two is unclear, and so the expression of a negative or positive attitude to, for example, the French may refer either to the people or to the language. Attitude scales have been widely used in applied linguistics to study **motivation** in SLL. In many such studies the **matched guise technique** has been used, itself based in part on Osgood's semantic differential.

language attrition Language loss in individuals and in communities. In the individual loss takes several forms: (a) loss of a later-acquired language through lack of use (the so-called 'first in last out' rule or the Rule of Ribot); (b) loss of a first language through lack of use, a common experience of migrant communities, and through ageing and accident: this may become pathological loss in conditions such as Alzheimer's, or, in the case of accident, **aphasias**; and (c) loss of a language only partially acquired, usually at school: this hardly justifies the label 'loss' since so little has typically been acquired. In the community, the loss of a language normally means that the community is declining in numbers, has been or is in process of being marginalised, and is in close proximity to an **LWC** which is taking over the community's public and, in due course, private functions, in a process of community **language shift**. Taken together, these various types of language loss may be regarded as language attrition.

language awareness Language awareness (a better title, which is sometimes used, is linguistic awareness) refers to metalinguistic understanding of language in general. Inevitably, such metalinguistic understanding has to be channelled through a particular language, or a small number of languages, but it is meant to have universal application. Secondary school syllabuses of language awareness have been developed, the idea being that an educated person should possess linguistic **knowledge** (such as what a **grammar** is, how language interacts with politics, how tonal languages differ from non-tonal ones) and that such knowledge is beneficial to **language learning**. To date there is no evidence to support this latter proposition. See also **metalanguage**.

language contact Languages are said to be in contact when they influence one another (as evidenced by, for example, lexical borrowing), the influence usually being largely one way. Thus Malay has influenced English (words such as *amok*) but there is much greater influence of English on Malay. Language contact is welcomed in some cases: it is said that one of the strengths of English is its very large **vocabulary**, a product of its openness to other languages; and in some cases opposed: until recently French fought hard against the intrusion of English terminology. Language contact comes about through geographical proximity (England and France, Wales and England), although such proximity may be resented and the language contact resisted (Germany and France). But resistance tends, as in the French–English case, to be official and may have no effect on individual choices. Contact also comes about through political intervention, especially colonialism (Latin in Western Europe), and through economic incursions. A current example is American globalisation, which brings with it an American English language influence. This influence extends English language learning and, in part, introduces American terminology into the languages of the countries experiencing globalisation. See also **lexis**.

language corpus A **text** collection containing many millions of running words sampled from large numbers of individual texts. It is computer readable, accessible with software, such as **concordances**, which can find, list and sort linguistic patterns. The corpus is designed for linguistic analysis so as to provide a set of descriptions of a **language variety** sampled on the basis of some sociolinguistic theory. Some scholars maintain that language corpora can provide richer language data than **informants** ever could, but doubting voices point out that corpora, however widely sampled, may still by chance omit vital information, for example the name of one day of the week.

language death Language death occurs when a **language** no longer has any **native speakers**. The language itself may continue in some form, as, say, Latin does in the Roman Catholic church. But Latin is still considered a dead language and not a living one. There is a point, a tipping point, at which a language starts to decline; it is then dying and it is unlikely that its death can be averted. Quite where that tipping point is remains unclear. Nowadays it may be when there is official recognition that the language is in decline and institutional efforts are put in place to arrest the death through **language maintenance**. Already it is probably too late and a simple rule of thumb could be that living languages wash their own faces. Signs of decline are easily noted: the acculturation of proper names (for example, in Wales the English 'David' replaces the Welsh 'Dafydd'), the replacement of a distinctive phonemic system, the loss of morphological features (for example, Latin case endings in the Romance languages) and their replacement by syntactic reorganisation, and the reduction of phonemic tones (as in Mandarin and Cantonese). See also **gender, native speaker, phonology, syntax.**

language decline The stage at which a language is losing more speakers than it is gaining. This is therefore indicative of approaching **language death.**

language distance The extent to which languages have similar linguistic features. Those language that belong together historically (for example the Germanic languages) appear to have more in common. It is claimed that language distance contributes to the ease or difficulty in **SLL**: thus French speakers should find Spanish easier to acquire than do English speakers.

language event Any discrete situation involving language. Since most situations involve language interactions, the term signifies that it is the language that is the focus of interest.

language for academic purposes see **LAP**

language in education There are two ways in which this term is used. The less common refers to the teaching of second languages in schools and colleges etc. Such educational practice is more commonly referred to as 'languages in education'. Whether language or languages, the activity is troubled, especially in anglophone countries where there is less and less emphasis on the teaching of languages in the **curriculum.** Conversely, but for the same reason, in non-anglophone countries, since the teaching of English dominates just about everywhere today, there is similarly less and less provision for a range of languages other than English (**LOTE**). The argument is complex; if, after all, language is intended primarily for **communication,** there is perhaps no need to teach any language other than English. If, on the other hand, language is intended for understanding, then perhaps we do need other languages. Economics and politics are also opposed: economically it makes sense to aim for an economy of scale, and teach (and train teachers and develop **teaching materials**) only in English. Politically, this is anathema to many non-anglophone countries, where such emphasis is regarded as hegemonic. Language in education more commonly refers to the role of language in the curriculum (this time it is language in the singular): this refers to the ways in which language enters into, aids and complexifies the teaching and learning of every subject. We say 'language' here but in reality this means giving greater prominence in schools and colleges to the first language (L1), or more accurately to the language which is the **medium of instruction**. Such programmes have been brought together under the heading of 'language across the curriculum', which was very active in the 1980s, less so now. Language in education also refers to another concern, the teaching of linguistic **knowledge** in the secondary school. This relates to the concern for language awareness, and is practised by those who wish to see wider understanding of linguistics and to encourage university study of the subject by preparing the ground in the high school, where a number of popular academic disciplines are fostered (e.g. maths and history). Of course there are other subjects which, like linguistics, do not have that lead-in, subjects such as psychology and engineering. See also **hegemony, language awareness.**

language laboratories The availability of cheap tape recorders in the 1960s made possible richer opportunities for teaching the oral component of a target second language, including self-access learning. Language laboratories were rooms with tape recorders, controlled from a central console which permitted the teacher to direct, assist and correct students' exercises and, in the advanced cases, enabled students to interact with one another and operate an audio-visual programme. Later development and elaboration of computer hardware seem to have made language laboratories redundant: computerised language learning allows self-access, does not need a special laboratory and can provide inter-action with other learners anywhere. As can mobile telephones. See also **audiolingual, CALL.**

language learning A term that conveniently distinguishes first and second language learning, whereby **first language acquisition** (also **child language acquisition**) is distinguished from **SLL.** A further distinction is also sometimes made: formal second language learning is known as SLL while informal learning is termed acquisition. However, **research** into the learning of second languages is widely known as second language acquisition research (**SLAR**).

language loss Loss by an individual of a first or of a second language, or loss by a community of its traditional language. See also **language attrition.**

language maintenance The attempt to avert **language death.** Language maintenance is typically a project instituted by some official body to provide teaching (including language-medium classes), written materials and other opportunities for people to hear, speak and then use the language. In its extreme form it mandates the use of the language being maintained (such as Irish in Ireland, Welsh in Wales) in various official functions. The recognition of this need for maintenance may indicate that **language decline** has already gone too far. See also **medium of instruction**.

language planning This operates in two modes, the macro and the micro. Macro language planning is referred to as status planning and involves legislation concerning the **official language(s)**, educational **curriculum** choices, and provision for **minority language** including issues concerned with language maintenance, revival and shift. Micro language planning, referred to as corpus planning or language engineering, concerns the modernising treatment accorded to a language so as to make its **grammar** and **vocabulary**, including its **discourse**, suitable for current use in a post-industrial and globalised world. What this means is that corpus planning is most evident in developing societies, where a colonial language has been the official language and the **medium of instruction** in education, while the local language(s) has or have been little used for scientific and technical writing. The decision to make the local language the official language demands that work be done to make the new official language fit for modernity. Malaysia is a case in point. Corpus planning has a long history and covers the work of national academies such as the French Academy, founded in the seventeenth century, as well as that of other bodies such as university publishers and the BBC, all contributing to establishing norms for a standard language and in doing so promoting corpus planning. The history of prescriptivism and the notion of **correctness** for the language and its presentation are relevant here. See also **prescription**.

language proficiency hypothesis In **bilingual education** programmes, this predicts that proficiency in the target language (Ly) determines reading ability in that target language (Ly). In contradistinction, the transfer of skills hypothesis predicts that what determines reading ability in the target language (Ly) is reading ability in the source language (Lx). See also **language proficiency tests.**

language proficiency tests Tests of **ability** in a language for some purpose(s) outside the language, in contrast to a language **achievement** test, which tests language ability for its own sake. Thus a proficiency test in English such as **TOEFL** or **IELTS** is intended to determine whether, for example, **non-native speaker** students have adequate English to undertake university education in the medium of English. Unlike an achievement test, a proficiency test is not based on a particular course of instruction. In spite of their world-wide **standardisation**, proficiency tests normally have a particular situation in mind: TOEFL is still primarily relevant to those who wish to study in the USA, and its use of **American English** is therefore justifiable. Established proficiency tests such as TOEFL and IELTS generate **washback** on instruction in the shape of preparation courses and textbooks oriented towards the test. In this way, they come to be used more and more as achievement tests. This achievement–proficiency dynamic leads to new proficiency tests being designed. See also **language proficiency hypothesis, testing.**

language programmes Projects mounted with new **teaching materials** and sometimes new **methodologies**, intended to revitalise **second language teaching.**

language rights The extension of human rights, such as the right to free speech and free assembly etc., extended to language. This represents the right to identify with one's first language, to maintain it and to develop it fully.

Acknowledged as a fundamental individual right, this is the position adopted by those who take a **linguistic imperialism** view of English. But in recent postcolonial discussions the concepts of **heteroglossia** and **hybridity** have been put forward to challenge the claims of language rights proponents that **linguicism** is destroying languages and cultures. See also **culture**.

language shift The process whereby a community (minority, migrant, isolated) abandons its first language in favour first of **bilingualism** and then of a new L1, that of the majority community. Shift takes place first in public domains (sometimes with the exception of religious discourse) until the only surviving domain is the intimate family setting. Language shift once started is difficult, perhaps impossible, to reverse and leads to **language death**. See also **language maintenance**.

language standards This term is used in two ways:
(a) to refer to the outcomes expected following a course of **language teaching**. These are typically presented as a list of statements which may be set out in the form of a scale, for example a 9-point scale, where the 9 means that the standards have been fully met.
(b) to refer to a code of ethics or of practice which sets out the standards which the **profession** (language teachers, language testers etc.) judges itself by. See also **codes, scales**.

language teacher education A nice example of ambiguous bracketing; but the sense we are concerned with here is the education of language teachers. To an extent this depends on the level at which they are teaching: the teacher of a 5-year-old has different needs from a teacher at university level. However, they both need near-native proficiency in the **target language, knowledge** of the linguistic systems (for example **grammar**), and a meta-linguistic awareness of how language is structured and how it is used. They need to know how to analyse their students' **accents** phonetically so that they can diagnose problems and provide remedial opportunities in **pronunciation**, including rhythm and **intonation**. University teachers are more likely to be called on for remedial work. All teachers need an understanding of how languages are learnt and what they are used for both cognitively and socially. In other words, they need a training in **applied linguistics**. The two groups differ in that the teacher of young children must pay attention to the development of early language learning, while the university teacher needs knowledge of how **language varieties** relate to one another and of development, and of the how and why a **standard language** evolves. In addition, of course, the university teacher will need to have read widely in the literature of the target language and in its history, themselves examples of **language's varieties**. Many, perhaps most, of those who attend postgraduate courses in applied linguistics are involved in or will in future be involved in language teacher education. It is not surprising therefore that the needs of language teacher education influence the content of training in applied linguistics. See also **metalanguage, SLAR.**

language teaching A term, like 'history teaching' or 'maths teaching', to mean the teaching of a language. It is used widely for second, foreign and classical language teaching. It is also, less frequently, used for the teaching of the first language, although there it may be more common to speak of partial areas (the teaching of reading, the teaching of writing, the teaching of literature). How far the teaching of language and the teaching of, say, history deserve to be considered parallel and similar activities is unclear. Institutionally they are treated as if they were equivalent, but it is likely that, because language teaching requires a huge investment in skills acquisition, it is music rather than history that provides language teaching with a parallel.

language testing The activity of developing and using language tests. As a psychometric activity, language testing traditionally was more concerned with the production, development and analysis of tests. Recent critical and ethical approaches to language testing have placed more emphasis on the uses of language tests. The purpose of a language test is to determine a person's **knowledge** and/or **ability** in the language and to discriminate that person's ability from that of others. Such ability may be of different kinds, **achievement**, **proficiency** or **aptitude**. Tests, unlike scales, consist of specified tasks through which language abilities are elicited. The term 'language assessment' is used in free variation with 'language testing', although the former is also used somewhat more widely, to include, for example, classroom testing for learning and institutional examinations. The activity of language testing is carried out by language testers, few of whom are engaged full-time in the activity. They may also be (they usually have been) language teachers and sometimes applied linguists. However, while **applied linguistics** claims language testing as an applied linguistics activity, it is less common for language testers to see themselves as applied linguists. See also **critical language testing**.

language use A language is a set of rule-governed systems (phonological, grammatical, semantic, discoursal and so on) which are put to use. They are used by those who control them, however partially, for a range of purposes from the most public and formal (taking an oath, a wedding ceremony, a legal contract) to the most personal (a family conversation, lovers' intimacies). It is interesting that at both extremes we find more ritualised and formulaic utterances. **Creativity** and originality thrive in the middle ground. In the mid-twentieth century, language use was largely the concern of applied linguists and other applied scholars. More recently, with the decline of the authority of the Chomskian theories, linguistics and linguists have become more involved in language use and the data it provides for their (often) functional theories.

language variety The term 'variety' is used very widely, ranging from a **language** as a variety to a **dialect**, a **register**, a field-specific use, even a **style**. Any language use which can be shown to be systematic and not random may be called a variety. The term is therefore useful if indefinable. See also **ESP**.

languages for specific purposes see **LSP**

languages other than English see **LOTE**

langue The French word for **language**, used by Saussure to refer to the language system shared by the social community. For Saussure, language was a social fact, held together tightly in a system that no individual could change. What does change is **parole** (= speech); if the community accepts the change then that causes the system (language) itself to change. Saussure's idealisation of a homogeneous community, all members sharing the same langue, is mirrored in Chomsky's concept of the ideal speaker/hearer: in his concept the **competence** of the individual parallels the langue of society and the individual's **performance** parallels society's parole. Saussure's construct helps explain how it is that **native speakers** somehow manage to interact intelligibly with one another, but his langue–parole distinction has been challenged, especially by corpus linguists who insist that there is no need for the distinction, since **language use** is itself both creative and patterned.

LAP language for academic purposes; the approach of **EAP** extended to other languages. Note that at present much, if not most, academic writing is in English and therefore the notion of English as occupying a unique role is easily understood. To a large extent therefore at present LAP = EAP. See also **academic discourse**.

learnability hypothesis (also **teachability hypothesis**) The hypothesis that instruction in some areas of **language** can accelerate the rate of learning but not cause learners to skip a natural stage. What it will do, it is claimed, is to move learners rapidly to the next stage of learning.

learning strategies The qualities that characterise successful language learners. They are, above all, strategies for active involvement. **Research** indicates four broad categories of learning strategies: metacognitive strategies (for example planning one's learning time); cognitive strategies (for example techniques for memorising **vocabulary**); affective strategies (for example ways to deal with frustration and increase **motivation**); social strategies (for example forming a group and pretending to understand). One aim of this research is to help less successful learners, although, as is obvious, the strategies that help one learner will not necessarily suit another.

learning style There are cognitive and affective dimensions to learning style. On the one hand there is an individual's preferred way of processing information and on the other her or his preferred way of dealing with other people. **SLAR** has focused on the distinctive learning style of field dependence and field independence. Those who are field dependent see things holistically and so do not identify the parts that make up a whole. But they find social interaction easy and interesting. Those who are field independent see things more analytically but they are also less inclined to social interaction. The hypothesis that field-dependent people learn better in informal **language learning,** and field-independent persons do better in more formal learning, has some support in the **research** literature. The application of learning styles to teaching is fairly straightforward but its efficacy does depend on whether learning styles themselves are found to be authentic.

lect Another name for **language variety,** hence **idiolect, sociolect, dialect.** Both 'lect' and 'variety' refer equally to geographical and social dialects.

LEP limited English proficiency; one of the terms used to denote second language learners of English. Others are **EFL, ESL** and **NESB.** Since such terms are predicated on absence, they are regarded as being negative and demeaning to non-English speakers: hence the terms **ESOL** and **LOTE.**

lexicography The art and craft of writing a **dictionary.** Lexicography depends for its analysis and selection on the prior work and research of **lexicology.**

lexicology The study of the **vocabulary** items (lexemes) of a language, including their meanings and relations and the changes in their **form** and **meaning** through time. See also **lexicography**.

lexis The **vocabulary** of a **language** (including both words and phrases), the antonym of **grammar**.

Likert Scale A particular type of ordinal **scale**, typically used in questionnaire analysis to gauge the comparative magnitude of respondents' **attitudes** or attributes. Respondents are invited to record the strength of their agreement with a series of assertions, such as: 'The test was a fair measure of reading ability', 'There was enough time allowed', 'The instructions were confusing', 'The text was difficult.' Responses are usually expressed on a 5-point scale in terms of these five categories: Strongly Agree, Agree, Undecided, Disagree, Strongly Disagree. Scoring is on the basis that a favourable response (Strongly Agree) is awarded a 5 and an unfavourable one (Strongly Disagree) a 1. Favourable and unfavourable statements are often interspersed to avoid a halo effect. Scores from the questionnaire are summed to produce an attitude or attribute score for each respondent. The Likert Scale (named after its inventor) is easier to administer and analyse than either the Thurstone Scale or the Guttman Scale, and is often used in **language programme** evaluation studies.

limited English proficiency see **LEP**

lingua franca A language which is used for **communication** between speakers who have no native language in common. Any language may therefore operate in this regard. A **pidgin** is a particular variety (see **language varieties**) of a lingua franca. See also **EliF**.

linguicism A theoretical model which proposes that there is systematic pressure by **LWC** and more particularly by languages of international reach on minority and poorly resourced languages, whereby, as in economic globalisation, the larger languages drive out the minority languages. This structural inequality between the more and the less powerful languages is, it is claimed, increased and maintained by those in **power**, whether deliberately or not is unclear. See also **linguistic imperialism**.

linguistic imperialism A subtype of **linguicism**. Phillipson offers this working definition of linguistic imperialism: 'The dominance of English is asserted and maintained by the establishment and continuous reconstitution of structural and cultural inequalities between English and other languages.' The idea of linguistic imperialism has received both interest and considerable approval as an explanation and an **ideology** to be combated. It has also attracted criticism on the grounds that **language shift** is a by-product of economic and political forces, that languages in contact have always operated thus, and that non-English speakers seeking English (or Cantonese speakers in Hong Kong now seeking to learn Mandarin) are not passive dupes but active decision makers, who view English or Mandarin as necessary to them for instrumental reasons. See also **hybridity, language contact, linguicism**.

linguistic persuasion The use of standard forms as a demonstration of status.

linguistic relativity (also the **Sapir-Whorf hypothesis**) The linguistic correlate of relativism, that long-established philosophical view that there is no universally shared understanding of the world. Individual perceptions are in part combined through social groupings. Thus common **cultures** provide a shared view of the world which members of a culture are socialised into accepting. So too for **language**, as argued by Edward Sapir and his pupil, Benjamin Lee Whorf. They maintained that language is also a coming together of individual understandings. So far there is little to dispute: indeed, so bland a statement sounds quite Saussurean. But Sapir and Whorf go further. They argue (or seem to argue: their writings are somewhat contradictory) that a common language provides both cognitive and affective coherence such that language group A (Whorf cites the American Indian Hopi people) categorises the world quite differently from language group B (Whorf suggests Standard Average European, which seems to mean English); and even further, that in doing so, the two groups have distinct perceptions of the world. The view is attractive because it seems to offer an explanation for **miscommunication** internationally and also to provide support for **language maintenance**, especially of small and declining languages, which, according to the hypothesis, must have a unique view of the world. The hypothesis has been severely challenged, partly by those who take a very different philosophical position, such as universalism, and partly because it does not lend itself to falsification. The strong Sapir-Whorf position would deny **SLL** and **translation**. And so a widely held position is the weak linguistic relativity position: yes, there are differences, yes languages categorise differently, but there are ways of creating understandings, and in any case these differences are more true of surface appearances.

linguistics The academic study of **language**, held by some scholars to be a science and by others a humanity. The modern development of philology, linguistics covers a large number of fields such as descriptive linguistics, historical linguistics, **phonetics/phonology**, **socio-linguistics**, **psycholinguistics**, **applied linguistics**, **anthropological linguistics** and **forensic linguistics**. A continuing and unresolved issue is how far these different fields belong together and whether linguistics *tout court* is a core discipline with which the others cohere as subdisciplines. This is particularly the case for applied linguistics, since, on the face of it, its only parent is linguistics, unlike, say, sociolinguistics, which has two parents, linguistics and sociology. Hence the attempts, so far unavailing, to convert applied linguistics into **educational linguistics**.

linguistics-applied The view that **applied linguistics** consists of the application of linguistics (narrowly defined) to real-world problems of **language use**, the main purpose being to validate a linguistic theory, using **real-world data** rather than laboratory or invented or speculative data.

literacy Literacy is often regarded as the ability to read. But the problem remains of what is selected as the criterion of reading; that is, the ability to read what and the ability to read with how much understanding (and possibly the ability to read how quickly)? Therefore, literacy is more carefully defined in terms of some literacy (or reading test) level. Levels of this kind are commonly converted into years of education and so there are literacy levels for primary, secondary and academic students. Literacy is also used more widely to include **writing** and indeed other language skills such as speaking, and even more widely to encompass the ease with which an individual operates in the social world. Literacy, therefore, like **grammar, culture** and **discourse**, is a useful, vague term which can be used to take account of complex social systems and the individual's place in them.

literary studies Literature, both oral and written, reflects an emphasis on **language** for its own sake. Literary **texts** are examples of **creativity** (like all art, music, painting, sculpture, dance) which uses language to provide its meanings. As such the focus is on the language, its **style** and its formal properties, and not on what functions, reporting, arguing, describing it conveys. Literature, therefore, has no purpose other than itself. Until fairly recently (indeed still today in some contexts) literature studies formed the basis for all **language learning**. Challenging, indeed admirable as such an approach is, deriving as it does from the studies of the classics (Latin and Greek), it is not satisfactory when larger and larger numbers are studying languages for specific and often instrumental reasons. At the same time, for many, literature is enjoyable and can therefore be used to attract language students by offering imaginative release from the hard graft of instrumentality.

longitudinal studies The kind of **research** design that is regarded in medical research as the gold standard, whereby the experimental sample (half receiving the treatment and half the placebo) are followed up over a long enough period to determine whether the treatment has had the effect claimed for it. In **applied linguistics** research there is rarely the time or the money available for such thorough research, and therefore compromises are normally made. It may also be the case that because it is so difficult in language studies to avoid contamination by external variables, longitudinal studies may not be wholly desirable. See **cross-sectional studies**.

LOTE (the teaching of) languages other than English. This Australian term is used of modern languages provided in the Australian education system. 'LOTE' is preferred to 'modern languages' because it confirms that English is also part of the language provision. Compare the US/UK acronym **TESOL**, which is used to demonstrate that English is one language among others.

LSP languages for specific purposes; the extension of the principles and procedures used in **ESP** to other languages. Usually these are modern languages, although there is no reason why a classical language such as Greek or Sanskrit could not be taught using a LSP model.

LWC languages of wider communication. LWC are **lingua francas** that operate outside their own region, often across a continent, but do not have international provenance. Thus English and probably still French are international languages. Spanish perhaps, German, Swahili, Russian, Arabic, Chinese, Hindi and Bahasa Malay (Indonesian) may be thought of as lingua francas. But the term is non-theoretical: it is both vague and wide. It appears not to include **pidgins** and other forms of business languages, although an LWC may in time foster the development of a pidgin.

M

markedness The view that less frequent (basic, natural) linguistic elements are marked whereas the more frequent (etc.) elements are unmarked. This has been applied to **grammar**: normal sentence order in English (subject-verb-object – SVO, for example: the boy kicks the bucket) is unmarked, while a less common order (object-subject-verb – OSV, for example: the bucket the boy kicks) is marked. It has also been applied to **phonology** (consonants such as p/t/k/s/n are said to be unmarked because they occur in most languages).

Marxism and language The influence of Marxism on ideas about **language** has been considerable. Tenets such as 'All signs are ideological in their very nature'; 'language is a central site for the class struggle'; 'language and politics are inseparable, perhaps even indistinguishable'; 'language is fundamentally dialogic and not monologic'; 'language is what keeps people apart'; 'linguistic analysis is mere abstraction unless it starts off from the recognition that its data consist of politically contextualised utterances' all show Marxist influence. Hence the insistence on Marxist inspiration in **critical discourse analysis**, which has an intellectual if not a political Marxist pedigree. There is a curious ambiguity in Marxist attitudes towards **standard language** in that, on the one hand, standard languages are tools of class dominance, while, on the other, the global spread of a standard language such as English can be seen to break down nationalistic ideologies that stand in the way of class consciousness. See also **ideologies**.

matched guise technique A technique to measure **language attitudes** which claims to control speaker difference/ effect. The technique was developed in Montreal by Lambert in the 1960s to study the attitudes of anglophones and francophones to each other's **language**. Speakers with native-like **proficiency** in both languages were recorded speaking translated texts in the two languages. Judges (both anglophone and francophone) were then invited to listen to the tapes and rate what they heard on various scales (such as friendliness, reliability, cooperativeness, religiosity, humour). The judges believed they were responding to two speakers, one francophone and the other anglophone, whereas in fact they were hearing two guises of the same person. The intention was to remove the factor of speaker **personality**, but doubt has been cast on the assumption that speaker personality can be discounted on the grounds that any two voices (of the same person or of two different persons) are likely to evoke the same stereotyped responses. If that is so, of course, then the complexity of the technique may not be necessary and the voices of two different speakers, matched by age, sex and educational background, would do just as well. Even so, the matched guise technique has been used very widely across a range of languages and situations, including clinical ones.

meaning What a **language** expresses by the use of its structure is its meaning. It is said to be the purpose of language to enable us to express the way we see the world. Word and sentence meaning are studied in **semantics, discourse** and **text** meaning in **discourse analysis,** in CA and in studies of **comprehension.** But meaning is still wider; indeed, it tends to escape all categorical boundaries, since it could be said that all life is about meaning. Certainly, **pragmatics** and functional theories are interested in kinds of meaning. The basic opposition between schools and **methodologies** of **language teaching** may be said to be between the structural (**grammar–translation**) and the communicative (semantics). Some linguists (for example Halliday) are unwilling to accept a distinction between **form** and **function**.

medium In applied linguistics, the **language** or **language variety** in which public activities (the workings of parliament, the law courts, education) take place.

medium of instruction The main language of instruction at school and college. In most cases the medium of instruction is the (**official**) **language** of the region or state. In areas of conflict where language is a divisive force, the medium of instruction can be a contentious issue (for example, between English and Bahasa Malay in Malaysia in the 1970s, and between Catalan and Castilian during the Franco period). As well as political and social arguments about the medium of instruction, there are psychological claims in support of the **mother tongue** being used as the medium of instruction, notably that of **BICS** and **CALP**.

men's language see **women's language**

mental lexicon The store in the memory of words and phrases. This appears to include knowledge of word endings and of the metaphorical function. One interesting question relates to the stability of the lexicon: whether, as new words enter, old ones survive or are turned out. See **lexicology, metaphor**.

mesolect see **acrolect**

metalanguage The language used to analyse or describe a **language**; also the capacity of language to refer to itself. With regard to the word, the piece that follows in square brackets is in metalanguage [in 'runs' the 's' indicates third person singular present]. Metalinguistic knowledge can be held with or without the metalanguage to describe it. See **language awareness**.

metaphor A word or phrase used for special effect, which deliberately denies its usual or literal meaning. For maximum effect it is necessary for the readers or inter-locutors to be aware that what they read or hear is a fiction, even though they may not be able to retrieve the original sense. A lover's cry of 'I am consumed with jealousy' is a metaphor even if the hearer is not aware what the literal meaning of 'consumed' is. Much of literature is metaphorical and yet metaphor, like jokes, remains a difficult area for second language learners even at an advanced level. **Critical discourse** analysts argue that it is the role of **applied linguistics** to demystify what Lakoff has called the metaphors we live by, those expressions that appear to represent reality but in fact are language **constructs**. To an extent, these are so-called dead metaphors. See also **SLL**.

methodology Systematic approaches to a practical activity, usually used in **applied linguistics** to refer to **language teaching**. Methodology has to do with the planning and arrangement of objectives, **teaching materials** and **assessment** and may also include realia. Hence the array of methodologies in language teaching: structural methodology, **notional-functional methodology**, com-municative methodology. Since methodology in applied linguistics cohabits with **linguistics, semantics, phonetics** etc. it was once proposed that methodology deserved to be put on a higher (more theoretical) plane, that of methodics. The proposal did not take off.

migration Movements of people(s), whether voluntary – as

in emigration and subsequent immigration – or forced –
as in slavery, colonisation, the effects of commercial
markets and the creation of refugees – all have some
effect, often only temporary, on **language**. Permanent
migration leads over time to a language switch, either for
the host community (as in British and French former
colonies) to adopt the incomers' language or the reverse,
as in the adoption of Gaelic by the Normans in Ireland.
Such movements raise issues of maintenance and
attrition for the community and of **language loss** for the
individual. Recent curbs on migration have prompted
governments to introduce a language test for new
migrants. See also **IELTS, language attrition, language
maintenance, language testing.**

minority languages Minorities are determined in two ways,
by number and by the **power** and **status** (political,
economic, financial etc.) they have. Language minorities
tend to be low on both counts; thus Australian
aboriginal language communities are both low in
number and low in power. Imbalance is possible. Thus
a numerical minority can be a majority in terms of
power, for example the colonists in anglophone and
francophone Africa. But notice that in such case the 'low
in numbers' is a local artefact: if there had been no
anglophone and francophone blocs outside the African
colonies it is likely that colonial language dominance
would not have lasted so long. Power and status are
more important than numbers but they are relevant, it
seems, only where there are homelands elsewhere with
a numerical majority. The Swedish language in pre-
independent Finland exemplifies this. It appears that
mobile minorities can take over a local majority without
the benefit of a distant homeland majority, but only
if they are prepared to switch from their incoming

language to that of the new country's majority (for example the Vikings in Ireland).

miscommunication A misunderstanding which may occur for a number of reasons. Among **native speakers** who share similar backgrounds it is likely that miscommunication takes place because of overdetermination of (reliance on) background and **context,** whereby the hearer makes too many inferences about what is heard. Among **non-native speakers** the opposite is more likely, whereby the lack of shared background means that even a simple – and well-formed – request or appeal or question may not be understood because it has unfamiliar pragmatics or accentual features.

mixed languages An uneasy term. It is clear that many people use features of more than one **language** in their speech. This is particularly so in bilingual and multilingual households and communities. But are these mixed languages? That is to say, is the repertoire that is undoubtedly being put to use indicative of some stable **lect?** The term should not be applied to **creoles** and **pidgins** which have established a steady state. It may be more appropriate to speak of mixed language rather than languages.

mother tongue The language to which the child is first exposed 'at the mother's knee'. The term and concept exist in languages other than English (for example French *langue maternelle*). There seems to be no equivalent concept (or label) 'father tongue'. See also **native speaker.**

motivation Two types of motivation are said to be available in language learning: (a) instrumental: the desire to learn a language to get a job, pass an examination; and (b) integrative: the desire to learn a language in order to communicate with the speakers of that language. The distinction between the two types has been much discussed, leaving unclear how far they can in practice be distinguished. After all, I may choose to learn to speak under integrative motivation but intend to use the language in entirely instrumental ways, for example to wind up a contract. In **SLAR**, researchers refer to extrinsic motivation (that which students bring to the classroom) and intrinsic motivation (that which is generated in the classroom by the teacher and the **teaching materials**). Motivation accounts for only slightly less of the **variance** in learners' **achievement** scores than **language aptitude**. For teachers it has assumed a dominant role even surpassing that of language aptitude, no doubt because it is thought that aptitude is immutable while motivation can be altered and maximised in the language classroom.

multiculturalism How a state responds to cultural diversity, often (but not always) after large-scale immigration, as in Australia in the second half of the twentieth century. A policy of multiculturalism affords resources and protection to the rights, practices and languages of all groups, including educational provision to make that policy active. Multiculturalism is a much vaguer (and therefore perhaps more successful) policy than **multilingualism**. See also **culture, migration**.

multilingual education The policy that follows from **multiculturalism** and **multilingualism**. Like those, it is very expensive. Where applied, it takes the form either of (some) local choice of, for example a second language to study at school (as in Australia), or of each language in the array of choices in the polity being used in one geographical location (as in South Africa and India). In the limiting case of **bilingualism** (minimal multilingualism), for example in Canada, there is no choice.

multilingualism The **language** policy based on a political acceptance of **multiculturalism**. It makes provision in official institutions such as the law and education for the full use of those languages recognised as being group languages within the state. There are three obvious problems with this policy. First, it can be very costly (as shown by the recent implementation in the enlarged European Community of interpreting into and out of all member state languages). Second, it is not clear at what point (numerical? economic?) a group's language should be given official recognition. And third, it creates huge inertia such that most of the recognised languages will have minimal use, while one, two or three dominant (international, ex-colonial) languages will be used for the whole range of official and public issues. India and South Africa offer examples of the courage needed to mount a policy of multilingualism and the problems that the policy is likely to encounter.

mutual intelligibility The extent to which speakers of Lx understand speakers of Ly. This may be a matter of degree, connected to the **language distance** between the two languages. Thus Swedish speakers are said to understand speakers of Norwegian more than they understand speakers of Danish. But mutual intelligibility may be affected by factors unrelated to language distance. Factors such as the **status** and **power** of the speakers of one language may cause the speakers of the less powerful language group to insist that there is mutual **intelligibility** between their language and that of the dominant group. Presumably, what has happened is that they have learnt the others' language. Contrariwise, speakers of the dominant community's language may insist that they do not understand the less powerful community's language even when they are (to an outsider) very close linguistically indeed. The relation between Urdu and Hindi has something of this imbalance. Another example might be metropolitan French and Quebecois French.

N

narrative Story telling, both spoken (oral narrative) and written (for example diaries). Labov has proposed a **genre** structure for narratives which has been widely taken up: abstract, orientation, complicating action, evaluation, result or resolution, coda. Control of these sequential phases of narrative would appear to be part of the learnt behaviour of the **native speaker**. As such, the ability to narrate has to be seen as a creative artefact and therefore not necessarily a representation (in the case of personal narrative) of actual events. See also **creativity**.

nation and language (A) **language** is one of the symbols commonly associated with belonging to (identity with) a nation. Brass proposes that in nation formation a pool of symbols is required, such as those of ethnicity, race, religion, language. It is therefore not surprising to find that many nations are associated in the minds of others (and indeed in their own minds) with one language (or a small number of languages). Indeed, it would seem difficult to establish or maintain a nation with no recognised 'national' language which is required for formal and official purposes. It is possible to establish more than one language as national, and then to select one (or two or three) as the official language(s). Thus in south Africa there are eleven national languages: nine African languages, Afrikaans and English. While provinces are free to choose which language is to be official at regional level, it seems that English is the language of choice in the state school system. We observe here a nice conjunction of the ideal (all eleven languages) and the pragmatic (English as the general choice). Since nations are to an extent **imagined communities,** the symbolic status of the nine African languages may well provide the necessary adhesive force to make nation identity a reality.

national language The language declared to be the main language of the nation; this may have more symbolic than actual meaning. The national language is usually also the **official language** (the language of government, law and administration). In certain cases, there may be more than one official language but only one national language. In Ireland, Irish Gaelic is the national language and the first official language; English is the second official language, and in practice the language most widely used in public and private **domains.**

nationalism The sentiment that a group of people form an entity which is extremely distinct and internally coherent. Such sentiment is important in nation building and makes use of powerful symbols such as those of **ethnicity,** religion, **language,** race. Dr Johnson referred to it in his dictionary (under the heading of 'patriotism') as 'the last refuge of a scoundrel'.

native speaker Everyone is a **native speaker** of the **idiolect** they acquire in early childhood. Through education they also gain access to the **standard language,** and it is their control of that standard language which normally defines them as native speakers of a particular language such as English. There is debate on how far advanced **proficiency** in Lx is a defining criterion or whether childhood acquisition is the only criterion that matters. There is further debate on how a native user of a **world English** such as Singapore English can be regarded as a native speaker. Related terms are home language, first language, **mother tongue** and dominant language.

naturalistic fallacy The linking of facts (is) and values (ought), the assumption that there is an ethics with which all must agree. **Critical applied linguistics** (and other critical approaches) seem to have fallen victim to the naturalistic fallacy.

needs analysis Determining the needs of language learners in a particular setting on the basis of situation, purposes, modalities and required **proficiencies**. Important in the planning of **syllabuses** and tests for **ESP** and **LSP**. See also **curriculum.**

negotiation Negotiation is a set of techniques employed unthinkingly by interlocutors in order to achieve **communication**. Breakdown in communication is avoided by the use of feedback, **foreigner talk** and **repair** at appropriate points in the **conversation,** the purpose being to continue the interaction unimpeded. Negotiation is thus a two-way process, as we see in the formal setting of diplomats engaged in attempting to resolve a political problem that is exercising their countries.

NESB Non-English-speaking background. This is the label attached in Australia to students from homes where the first language is not English; in Canada a related term is 'heritage language students'.

new variety of English see **world English(es)**

non-English-speaking background see **NESB**

non-native speaker see **native speaker**

non-Standard English Any systematic variation in terms of accent or dialect from Standard English.

norm The social reality of the **correctness** notions, the conventions in speech and writing of a **standard language**. While rules are linguistic, norms are social, thus **Australian English** and **British English** may be said to share the same rules but to have different norms.

notation see **transcription**

Nynorsk see **Bokmal**

O

observation A method used in **qualitative research** requiring the investigator to be physically present over time during the interactions of the subjects being researched. Data is collected by note-taking, diaries and now audio and video recording. Observation has traditionally been used in ethnographic research and in anthropological fieldwork where by long residence the investigator has (attempted to) become part of the community under observation. This practice, known as participant observation, is said to overcome the **observer's paradox**. See also **anthropological linguistics**.

observer's paradox In ethnographic research, the observer's presence may have an influence on the behaviour of those being observed and therefore the data collected will not be what Labov in his studies of **conversation** has called the **vernacular**. Whether the observer's presence really does affect behaviour is of course not open to investigation, since without that presence no data are collected. Various solutions have been proposed. One is that of participant observation; another (advocated by Labov) that the subjects can be shocked into forgetting that they are being observed by particular questions such as whether they have ever experienced the fear that they are about to die. And there is the unscientific view that (perhaps) people's behaviour does not change whether or not they are being observed. See also **observation**.

offensive language The use of swear words, taboo words and other -ist words (sexist, racist etc.) in situations where they may cause offence to others – hence blasphemy and obscenity – and may be illegal. Such terms typically refer to sexual practices, bodily functions, and religious or ethnic (including **gender**) matters. What counts as offensive appears to change over time; thus offensive language, like **language** itself, does not remain static. See also **political correctness**.

official language The language or languages used in a state for government and legal business. The official language is usually the **national language** but in multilingual states this may not be the case.

ontogeny The development of the human organism over time. One such model has been proposed by Piaget in his stages of development. For language acquisition the crucial stage appears to be the so-called **critical** (or sensitive) **period**. See also **phylogeny**.

orthography The term is used both for spelling in general and for correct (**Standard Language**) spelling. For languages regulated by Academy-type bodies (such as French), this is laid down; for others (such as English), this is a matter of educated usage. Orthography refers mainly to alphabetic writing. Other writing systems are syllabic and ideographic. See also **alphabetisation, writing, writing systems.**

output The necessary corollary to **input**, which on its own does not provide the practice needed for proficient use of a language. Full grammatical acceptance, it is suggested, develops only with the production of comprehensible and more accurate output.

P

paralinguistic Paralinguistic features are non-vocal phenomena which accompany speech (or may indeed replace it). They include facial expressions, head and eye movements, hand gestures and larger body movements.

parole The term used by Saussure to refer to concrete acts of speaking by individuals in actual situations. He distinguished this from **langue**, the language system shared by a community of speakers. Chomsky makes a similar distinction (albeit with a psychological slant) between **performance** and **competence.**

participant observation see **observation**

pedagogy The study (some would say the science) of teaching. The attempt to theorise a practical activity.

performance Distinguished by Chomsky from **competence**

and analogous to the Saussurean **parole**, performance refers to a speaker's actual use of language.

personality Reckoned to be a key element in explaining **individual differences** in **language learning**, through factors such as anxiety, risk-taking, tolerance of ambiguity, empathy, self-esteem, inhibition, and extraversion/introversion. The problem is what to do for those whose personality is not conducive to learning. While intervention may have an effect on **motivation**, it is difficult to see what can be done with **personality**.

phatic communion Language that lacks content and is used solely to establish and maintain social relations. The anthropologist Malinowski invented the term with reference to Pacific Islanders conversing about their gardens. In British English, interactions about the weather have an equally empty content. Much phatic communion consists of **ritualised routine** phrases.

philosophy of applied linguistics This may be understood in three senses: (a) a philosophically informed account of the nature of **applied linguistics** as well as the important landmarks in its development; (b) a philosophy-of-science approach to applied linguistics; and (c) a broad range of philosophically important issues that have come to concern applied linguists, such as the **ethics** of their **profession**.

phoneme The minimal unit in the sound system of a language. There are two main criteria for defining a phoneme, the first being complementary distribution. Sounds may belong to the same phoneme if they do not occur in the same position; thus in English the 'light' <l> sound always occurs before a vowel (e.g. <leaf>), and the 'dark' <l> is always final or followed by a consonant (e.g. <feel>). These two 'l' sounds are in complementary distribution. The second criterion is phonetic similarity. The two sounds <ng> and <h> are in complementary distribution in English (one never occurs in first position, the other never in last), but they do not sound alike. Unlike the two 'l' sounds, they are not allophones (or realisations) of the same phoneme.

phonemics Nowadays the term **phonology** is generally preferred.

phonetics The branch of **linguistics** that studies the whole range of sounds that the human vocal apparatus can produce, while the more theoretical **phonology** studies the sound systems of languages.

phonology The branch of **linguistics** which studies the sound systems of languages, while **phonetics** studies the whole range of sounds that the human vocal apparatus can produce.

phylogeny The development of the human species over time. Various models have been proposed, such as development from *Homo erectus* to *Homo sapiens*, from hunter-gatherer to pastoral. The emergence of **language** is seen to be a crucial stage in human development.

pidgin A language which develops as a contact language (for trade etc.) between speakers of different languages. Pidgins can develop a high degree of stability. See also **interlanguage**.

plagiarism Unattributed copying, often from well-known authors. Said to be on the increase with the growth of the internet. Students who plagiarise are considered to be guilty of an offence. In published material this is known as copyright violation.

plain English see **plain language**

plain language Written usage which tries to avoid overly complex structures and technical jargon. Associated with the Plain English movements, which advocate the **simplification** of official (especially legal and government) documents (see **Basic English**). Simplifying **texts** is by no means easy and in professional and specialist fields, jargon is probably necessary.

point of view The position from which the writer presents an idea or topic. Especially important in the **stylistics** of literature, where the writer may shift from one point of view to another.

politeness How language deals with the concept of **face** (maintaining a positive image of the self in conversation) and with its preservation given acts which are potentially damaging to it. Also concerns how languages express social distance between speakers. Languages differ in how they express politeness: in some this will be grammatical, in others by means of one or more words, and in yet others it may even be **paralinguistic**.

political correctness Used as a pejorative label for those who object to terms that are thought to be sexist, racist etc. Sometimes these remarks are directed at the use of non-sexist, non-racist terms (such as chairperson, humankind) which attempt to avoid discrimination, including made-up terms which mock those who are anti-discrimination and pro-inclusion, terms such as 'herstory' and 'womyn'.

positivism The theory that positive knowledge can only be based on experimental investigation and observation of natural phenomena. The term was introduced by the French sociologist August Comte in the nineteenth century. He maintained that human beings were suitable for scientific study (a revolutionary idea at the time) and therefore should be studied with more experimental rigour, with null **hypotheses** and statistical measures.

postcolonial societies Those countries that have become independent since World War II. Once independent, they were able to make their own decisions, including that of which **language**(s) to use for different purposes. The term 'postcolonial' is used in **applied linguistics** to refer to the common problems of such emerging societies, their difficulties in reaching **language planning** decisions and the pressures they face in the process.

postmodernism The contemporary sense of scepticism felt by scholars in the humanities and the social sciences with regard to progress, to the validity of **knowledge** and science, and generally to universal explanations and the optimism of the Enlightenment. This reinforces and explains the shift in **applied linguistics** from a more **quantitative research** paradigm to one that is more qualitative and seeks relative rather than universal explanations. Hence the emphasis on narrative research designs. Hence too the rise of **critical applied linguistics**. Postmodernism in language studies manifests itself particularly in **poststructuralism**, which rejects theoretical (top-down) approaches in favour of bottom-up ones, giving rise in applied linguistics to such developments as communicative approaches and constructivist arguments. See also **communicative language teaching**.

poststructuralism In **applied linguistics,** poststructuralism insists that **language** is a self-subsisting social entity wherein physical and mental images are brought into alignment without the need for any referent outside language. To an extent poststructuralism is a re-interpretation of Saussure's original theory of language as a significating rather than a representational phenomenon.

power Like money, power is the currency that those with valued resources have. Its citation so generally in **applied linguistics** indicates just how pervasive (and important) power is: thus we find it referred to in **discourse analysis, gender** studies, **language testing,** and the study of **language and the law, minority languages,** the **native speaker.** The resources in each case may be different, but in all cases the domination of power is constant: this language as medium in schools and law-courts, this gender's language use as more valid, this **dialect** as the language of test instruments etc.

pragmatic competence The ability required by both L1 and L2 speakers to use their linguistic resources in order to convey and interpret **meanings** in real situations, including those where they encounter problems due to gaps in their knowledge. In other words, such **competence** allows speakers to handle situations which they have never before encountered, a most difficult task for the L2 learner.

pragmatics The study of meaning in **context.** Unlike **semantics,** pragmatics therefore takes account of interlocutors and their communicative purposes. See also **pragmatic competence.**

prescription Presentation (to students and to the public more generally) of rules of **correctness** and of correct forms. Generally these are rules and forms that belong to the **standard language**, and may be out of date since the standard language itself changes over time. Prescription (like its negative associate **proscription**) is not popular, since it appears to restrict and limit free expression. But there is a sense in which both **dictionaries** and role models prescribe **usage**, if only implicitly, and it can be helpful to offer conventional (and accepted) ways of using language for those (indeed for all of us from time to time) who have questions or areas of uncertainty. Prescription is in practice a declaration of the **norms** that are current at any one time.

prestige Groups with **power** generally also have prestige, which in turn becomes attached to the **language** and the language forms they use. Thus **RP** has prestige, but so too do covert prestige **language varieties** such as that of Liverpool (by association with the Beatles) and that of Estuary English, the accent common to many young people in South London and adopted elsewhere because it seems chic. There is some evidence that females use more standard (and therefore prestige) variants than males. In attaching prestige to a **minority language**, informal promotion by creative writers and other artists seems to be important, though whether this deserves the title 'prestige planning' given to it by some scholars is unclear. See also **attitudes**.

prior knowledge Used as a variant of **background knowledge**, the general **knowledge** (of the world, language etc.) that speakers and readers bring to their **task**.

profession An activity requiring specialised **knowledge** and often long and intensive preparation or training, maintaining by force or concerted opinion high standards of **achievement** and conduct and committing its members to continued study and to a kind of work which has for its prime purpose the rendering of a public service. The 'force' requirement is seen very clearly in the medical and legal professions, which operate a 'licence to practise' system and have the authority therefore to exclude those whose professional conduct is deemed inappropriate. The extent to which **applied linguistics is** a profession is an open question. Since it lacks the authority to license and to sanction, the use of the term 'profession' remains aspirant.

proficiency **Ability** to use a language for a particular purpose; thus proficiency in English for academic study or to work in air-traffic control, proficiency in Japanese to operate as a tour-guide for Japanese visitors to Australia. Well-known **proficiency tests** of English (such as **TOEFL** and **IELTS**) do not lay down **syllabuses** on which students are tested: this is the province of achievement tests. Proficiency is also used more widely to refer to a general type of **knowledge** of or **competence** in the use of a language, regardless of how, where or under what conditions it has been acquired. See also **curriculum.**

pronunciation The production of a sound or set of sounds, with particular reference to the way in which the sounds are perceived by the hearer. It is also used to refer to the entire production of speech by an individual; thus 'I was (not) impressed by his/her pronunciation.' Effective pronunciation in an L2 brings together control of the **phonemic** system of the **target language** and the individual's conforming to an acceptable system of **phonetics.**

propaganda The systematic propagation of information and ideas by an interest group (such as a political party or government agency) so as to encourage a desired response among recipients and win support for the interest group. Propaganda may be written or spoken and typically makes use of untruths. See also **advertising**.

proscription The negative correlate of **prescription**.

psycholinguistics The study of **language** and the mind, how language is acquired, understood, stored and produced. The psychology of language is somewhat broader in scope, concerned with issues such as language and thought. Compare the relation between **sociolinguistics** and the **sociology of language**. See also **linguistic relativity, UG**.

Q

qualitative research Research that is not in numerical form, for example open-ended questionnaires or interview (or essay) data. Qualitative research may develop its own categories while the research is ongoing (and therefore is less likely to use pre-existing categories). As such it is thought to avoid at least in part the positivist assumptions of quantitative research. Qualitative research has links with **ethnography**. Although it appears very different from **quantitative research**, its data can be converted into quantitative form.

quantitative research Research that collects data in a numerical form, obtained through counting and measurement, for example test scores or data from fixed response questionnaires. Quantitative research is considered to reflect a positivist approach to research and therefore employs agreed categories and uses an empirical method. As such it assumes its research is scientific. This is disputed by those who claim either that the social sciences are not like the natural sciences or that the objects being researched (the phenomena of **applied linguistics**) are not necessarily observable. Quantitative research has links with psychology. Although it appears very different from **qualitative research**, its data can be converted into qualitative form.

queer theory Extends theories of **gender** in viewing sexuality as a complex array of social codes and forces, forms of individual activity and institutional **power** which are socially constructed.

R

readability The degree to which a given group of people find certain reading materials comprehensible. Readability formulae are the most widely used method for predicting **text** difficulty. Many of those in current use are based on only two factors, **vocabulary** (word frequency and length) and **syntax** (average sentence length). Attempts have been made to take account of important aspects of text difficulty, such as interest, compellingness, legibility (including typeface), conceptual load and organisation. These attempts have not been altogether successful, largely because of the problem of valid measurement of such factors. Among well-known readability formulae are the Dale-Chall, Bormuth, Fry and Gunning-Fog. However, in spite of their aim of assessing comprehensibility (that is, reader comprehension), what readability measures actually assess is relative difficulty among texts. It is to their failure to assess comprehensibility that we owe the development of the **cloze**

procedure. In spite of their limitations, readability formulae give a crude approximation to text difficulty and are reported to have reasonably high correlations with one another. They are fairly easy to compute. See also **comprehension, simplification**.

real-world data The use of real-world data in **language teaching** has a long tradition – both teachers and students have made use of diaries, newspapers, novels and so on, which belong to and originate from the world outside the classroom. But the modern use of the phrase 'real-world data' refers more particularly to the emphasis in some communicative models of language teaching (see **communicative language teaching**) on basing the whole learning experience on real **language use**; that is to say, on encounters and events that are very clearly not designed for deliberate **language learning** exercises. This is more easily achieved in advanced learning than in the early stages. Indeed, attempts to make early learning directly reflect the real world tend towards **ritualised routines**. In any case, the categorical separation of the classroom from the real world is surely a false distinction, since it suggests that learning is not part of the real world.

Received Pronunciation see **RP**

reflexivity In grammatical description this concerns a verb or construction where both subject and object refer to the same entity; thus in English, 'he washed himself'.

register A way of referring to an institutionalised **language variety**. Registers are linguistically distinct varieties in which the **language** is systematically determined by the **context**. Attempts to describe discrete registers such as the register of legal English have proved to be problematic because of the indeterminacy of the boundary between one field and another (say between geography textbooks and geology textbooks). See also **ESP, genre**.

relexicalisation see **delexicalisation**

reliability The extent to which a test measures consistently. Since without reliability there is no **validity**, reliability is a necessary but not sufficient quality of a test.

repair Ongoing error correction by speaker (self-repair) or interlocutor (other repair). See also **error analysis**.

research Systematic study of an event, problem or phenomenon, making use of an explicit **methodology** and designed to test one or more **hypothesis**.

restricted code Bernstein's term for one of the **language varieties** used to convey meaning in a social context. He claimed that those accustomed to the restricted code would have a more restricted **vocabulary** range, use more question tags, and use the pronouns 'he' and 'she' in place of nouns, while those using the **elaborated code** would make a greater use of adjectives, use a more complicated sentence structure and the pronoun 'I'. Although Bernstein was not specifically addressing the issue of language (since he was equally interested in **context** and social role), his work was wrongly interpreted as comparing the use of English of the working class (restricted code users) and of the middle class (elaborated code users). What those employing the elaborated code were capable of was removing themselves from their accounts, to write (and speak) generally rather than with reference to their own specific experience. Earlier names for the restricted and elaborated polarities were private and public.

rights (often **human rights**) Those rights (claims, needs, ideals) that individuals can properly expect to be provided by society, such as education, housing, work and freedom from oppression. Certain rights are regarded as being inalienable (such as the right to protect one's life and property) and others are said to be civil, that is, guaranteed under law. The aim of those promoting **language rights** (such as the right to **education** etc. in the **mother tongue**) is to convert what they see as a natural or inalienable right into a civil responsibility.

Riksmal see **Bokmal**

ritualised routines Prefabricated phrases that are used to convey an understanding of the **context** (and are therefore appropriate) rather than to offer specific information. Much **conversation** makes use of these routines. See also **phatic communion**.

romanisation The use of an alphabet type of **writing system**, either *ab novo* or by conversion from a **syllabic** or an **ideographic** script (for example Turkish and Vietnamese).

RP Received Pronunciation. Originally called Received Standard, this is the model of English **pronunciation** described by the phonetician Jones and codified in his *English Pronouncing Dictionary*. Essentially it is the pronunciation of southern England and more particularly of the famous public schools and the upper classes. It is said therefore not to be (unlike the other accents of English) regional. While RP is still heard, it is less common and probably less prestigious than it was. Nowadays, a modified RP (possibly with a suggestion of a regional **accent**) is esteemed, certainly if the newscasters and readers on the BBC are exemplars.

S

Sapir-Whorf hypothesis see **linguistic relativity**

scales In **language learning**, ways of grading the **ability** continuum from zero to **ultimate attainment** by establishing (and usually describing) a series of levels (or stages or way-stations). The scales contained in the European Common Framework are now widely used. In themselves scales are not measures but may be used as a component of a testing procedure and as a reporting method. See also **Council of Europe.**

schema theory A schema has been defined as an abstract structure representing concepts. It is stored in memory, and current usage suggests that **knowledge** of objects, of routine behaviour, and of belief systems all qualify as 'schemata'. The term has also been used to refer to the structure of **texts**, such as **narrative**, description, comparison etc. Given such general use, 'schema' is now regarded as a somewhat primitive (that is, non-theoretical) term and its place has been largely taken by **background knowledge.**

second language acquisition research see **SLAR**

second language learners Those acquiring (usually through formal study) a language which is not their **first language.** Thus the **target language** currently being acquired by a second language learner may be his or her third or fourth etc. language. All languages after the first language are second languages.

second language learning see **SLL**

second language teaching The formal teaching in an educational institution of a language that is not the learner's **first language**. All **language teaching**, other than that of the L1, is regarded as second language teaching even though some learners study more than one second language. Strong views are held about second language teaching, both by the profession and by the public, especially with regard to the best age to start a second language, the training required for second language teachers, and the role of the native-speaking teacher. Perhaps the most perplexing issue is how far **SLAR** can or should inform second language teaching. See also **age factors, SLL.**

secular linguistics The term used by Labov to refer to his quantitative approach to sociolinguistics. For proponents of this view, **sociolinguistics** offers a helpful methodology for mainstream **linguistics**, analysing real **language** in a real **context** and providing evidence for principles of linguistic change.

semantics The study of **meaning**, its purposes being to examine the systems of meaning available in Lx and how these differ from those in Ly, and to determine to what extent meaning can be explained as an extension of **grammar.**

semilingualism The popular notion that children growing up in a bilingual (or multilingual) environment never learn any one **language** fully and are therefore semilingual in both. This view has been discredited, but it is worth noting that in so far as access to the written language(s) is concerned, it does seem possible that those with no or partial education may be semilingual in that modality. The distinction therefore needs to be drawn between the social situation in which some children never gain full access to any (**standard**) **language** and the cognitive reality that utterly refutes the claim of semilingualism. See **bilingualism.**

sign languages see **ASL, BSL**

SIL Summer Institute of Linguistics. A Christian missionary organisation dedicated to making the Bible available to all through **translation** into local **vernaculars.** This mission has required the SIL to work on **writing systems** and translations in various locations, and in doing so has attracted to the task a number of well-known linguists.

simplification In **applied linguistics,** the process by which the language of reading materials is consciously adjusted for a group of learners so that they can understand the materials. Simplification refers to the selection of a restricted set of features from the full range of language resources for the sake of pedagogic efficiency. The code is not changed: what learners are presented with is a restricted sample of the full language system. A distinction has been made between simplified versions and simple accounts; simplified versions represent changes to an already existing text, while for simple accounts there is no pre-existing **text,** only a topic which is being rendered to suit a particular kind of reader. More broadly, simplification refers to the natural development of increasing regularity in a **language variety,** for example the loss of grammatical **gender.**

slang Language of a **colloquial** type, which changes with taste and fashion. It is often associated with particular age-groups in a society and is used by individuals partly to indicate membership of a group. Because such groups quickly change over time, membership has to be constantly reclaimed, hence the rapid turnover of slang terms. Slang words and phrases therefore belong to the spoken language: those items of slang that endure find their way into **writing**.

SLAR second language acquisition research. Systematic research into the learning of second languages. In recent years the field has grown substantially as an empirical and theoretical enterprise, the main focus of attention being on the difference, if any, between first and second language acquisition. The argument is that if different, SLAR can throw light not only on **language learning** but also on human cognition. How far developments in SLAR have (or can have) an impact on **second language teaching** and learning is an unresolved question. See also **first language acquisition, SLL.**

SLL second language learning. The practice and study of the learning and teaching of second languages. SLL has always attracted research interest, no doubt because while languages are undoubtedly important and desirable, it is difficult and time-consuming to achieve a proficient state. Hence the interest in different methods (the structural method, the communicative method), in starting age and in technological aids such as the **language laboratory** and **CALL**. To an extent decisions concerning SLL are political, in that its institutional programmes are typically politically driven; for example, the starting age for language study in a given polity, or the lack of a selective entry to a language course, are rarely decided on the grounds of research evidence but more usually on the grounds of political expediency. See also **SLAR**.

social class One of the fundamental types of social stratification, along with religious caste and political estates. The nineteenth-century growth of industrial capitalism encouraged the emergence of a class system, defined by Karl Marx and others largely in economic terms. The use of particular **accents**, **dialect** and even languages is considered a marker of social class, a connection made in literature (for example G. B. Shaw's *Pygmalion*) and in **sociolinguistics** by, for example, Bernstein.

social constructivism A general term that can be applied to theories that emphasise the socially created nature of social life and the idea that society is actively and creatively produced by human beings. In **applied linguistics**, social constructivists such as Lantolf take for granted that **language** is made or invented through **interaction**.

social identity The sense of self within a particular social **context**; since such contexts change over time and across place, so too does the individual's negotiations of his or her **identity**. For language learners, language plays a crucial role in this negotiation, giving (and denying) access to powerful social networks.

sociocultural theory Influenced by the writings of Vygotsky, sociocultural theory has informed **applied linguistics'** understanding of interaction. The notion of 'a zone of proximal development' reveals a pattern of development in which learners bring to interactions their own personal histories replete with values, assumptions, beliefs, rights, duties and obligations. The emphasis is on the learner's own agency informed by the care-giver's interaction. See also **social constructivism.**

sociolect A **language** variety (or **lect**) which is socially based rather than geographically. Typically associated with **social class.** See also **acrolect.**

sociolinguistic competence One of the aspects of **communicative competence,** this consists primarily of **knowledge** of how to use **language** appropriately in social situations.

sociolinguistics The study of the relationship between **language** and society. Its purpose is to further understanding of the nature of human language (rather than of society, as in, for example, **ethnomethodology**). Sociolinguistics includes such studies as **anthropological linguistics, dialect studies, discourse analysis, ethnography of speaking,** geolinguistics, **language contact** studies, **secular linguistics,** the social psychology of language and the **sociology of language.** In **applied linguistics,** the role of **language in education** is an important aspect of sociolinguistics.

sociology of language Also known as macro **sociolinguistics,** this deals with language choice and language intervention. It incorporates such studies as **language planning, multilingualism, language maintenance, language shift** and certain aspects of **language and education.**

speech act The smallest unit of analysis in conversational interaction. According to J. L. Austin's theory, there are three types of speech act: the locutionary act (the basic literal meaning of an **utterance**), the illocutionary act (what the speaker intends by the utterance) and the perlocutionary act (the actual effect the utterance has on the hearer). In **language teaching** and **syllabus** design, speech acts are sometimes referred to as **functions** or language functions. See also **curriculum**.

speech community A group of people of any size (a family, village, region, country etc.) who share, or believe they share, the same **language variety** or varieties. It is therefore possible to belong to a speech community without necessarily being fluent in the main language variety as long as one accepts it as dominant. The term 'speech community' is more a primitive (non-theoretical) than a theoretical term.

speech event A discrete **interaction**, often a conversation, bounded on both sides by silence and often marked by introductory and concluding remarks.

speech pathology (also known as **speech therapy**) The application of **clinical linguistics** to the study of language problems in child development and in ageing, illness and accidents. Speech pathologists (or therapists) diagnose disorders (such as stuttering and **aphasias**) and arrange for remedial treatment. See also **age factors**.

speech style The manner of speaking varying by **context** and interlocutor. The use of an appropriate speech style, which varies from frozen through formal, casual and colloquial to intimate, is part of a **native speaker**'s competence. The choice of an inappropriate style indicates humour or alienation or a language learner. See also **genre, register**.

stakeholders All those involved in or affected by **institutional language,** such as a **language planning** policy, a law, a **syllabus** and, heavily influenced by recent concerns about **ethics, language testing.** See also **curriculum.**

standard accent The **norms** of **standard language** properly apply to the written language. The extent to which similar norms apply to the spoken language is unclear. Certainly, there is widespread assumption that as far as **British English** is concerned, a version of the **accent** known as **RP** (formerly Received Standard) is the **prestige** accent, even today. However, prestige also belongs to other accents, such as educated Scottish English, and Estuary English. Furthermore, it is the case that other regional accents are acceptable (even if they lack prestige) in formal situations as long as the speaker is using the standard **grammar** and **vocabulary.** Prestige is also accorded covertly to accents such as Liverpool English because of the adulation given to the Beatles.

Standard English The written **dialect** of the educated, accessible to all through detailed codification (in **dictionaries,** descriptive grammars etc.), **education** and the normative practices of publishers and government institutions. There are several Standard Englishes: British, American, Australian and so on. But the actual differences, though marked, are minimal and interfere little with mutual **intelligibility.** A current debate concerns the status of so-called **world Englishes,** in particular those codes that have persisted in the non-settler ex-colonies (India, Malaysia, Nigeria etc.): the unresolved question is whether there is available a **standard variety** for any of these codes.

standard language The **dialect** of a **language** that has been

standardised and therefore has an agreed **writing system,** grammar and **dictionary**. In addition it is normally the variety used for official purposes, including education.

standard varieties Languages such as English and German offer a choice of a standard dialect: for English, British English, American English; for German, the German of Germany and the German of Austria etc. This is also the case for other languages such as Spanish and Portuguese, but, interestingly, apparently not yet for other languages such as French and Chinese, even though each has been adopted as the **official language** in more than one country.

standardisation The process by which a particular **dialect** is selected for official purposes, codified, accepted by the **speech community** and then (or at the same time) where necessary elaborated so as to fit it for use in contemporary society. See also **codification**.

standards The concept of and the concern for standards have a long tradition, sometimes under different names; the most common is probably **norms**, but there are other familiar terms too, such as 'rules' and 'conventions'. What they all indicate is that there are social goals and that there are agreed ways of achieving them. In language studies, apart from the common uses of standard in reference to (a) language – thus **standard language** (**Standard English**, Standard French and so on) – standards are ways of behaving, like conventions. Within institutions they have more authority since they can be used as non-negotiable goals, hence **benchmarks**, attainment targets, band-scales, profiles and competencies, all of which offer standards of **performance** with which learners' progress and achievement can be compared.

status The position a person occupies in society (for example, a doctor, a government minister, a plumber). To distinguish the sense of status from that of role, it is common to refer to a form of social stratification determined by legal, political and cultural issues. Thus, the higher the status (for example that of a member of the nobility or a judge) the greater the power. Examples of status groups are, at the higher end, conquerors or colonists and, at the lower end, slaves and the colonised.

stereotype Popular representations of the speech of particular groups (for example the **Australian English** realisation of day: /dai/), making use of a very small number of features and offering highly exaggerated accounts. Sterotyping often has a humorous intent but the features it seizes on are, in fact, typical if trivial. In **sociolinguistics**, the term 'stereotype' is used technically to refer to a linguistic variable which indicates both social and **style** stratification. See also **attitudes**.

stigmatisation The evaluation of a linguistic **form**, an **accent** or a **dialect** (or even a **language**) negatively because of its association with a lower-status group or community. Thus the use of the glottal stop in certain accents of English (as in /boʔl/ in Glasgow English) is perceived to be 'bad' even though the glottal stop occurs in other contexts in all English accents.

structural linguistics In a general sense, every school of **linguistics** can be termed structural, since linguistic features are typically described in terms of structures and systems. But there is a more restricted sense referring to the processes of classifying and segmenting the physical features of utterances. Such an approach is found in, for example, **systemic functional linguistics**, which has found favour with a number of applied linguists. For generative linguists (followers of the research paradigm developed in the 1950s by Noam Chomsky, and based on the concepts of an innate language factor and of **UG**), this approach is concerned only with the **surface structure**, while what is important in a language description is the underlying or **deep structure**. Structuralism has been hugely influential in the social sciences (notably in anthropology), where the network of relations constitutes the structures of a given system, their only meaning being the relations themselves.

structuralism The approach we observe in **structural linguistics**.

style Variation in speech or **writing** depending on social **context**. Style may also refer to the way of speaking or writing at a certain historical period (the Victorian period) or by a particular person, usually a named writer such as Shakespeare or Mark Twain. See also **speech style**, **stylistics**.

stylistics The study of the variation in **language** dependent on situation and on the intended effect of the writer or speaker. Stylistics is largely concerned with the study of the written language, particularly with literary **texts**, where the focus is on the reason for the writer's choices.

Summer Institute of Linguistics see **SIL**

superposed variety A **language variety** which is given precedence over local **dialects** because it has a particular social function and is usually itself a **standard variety**.

surface structure The structure of a sentence which a person actually hears or speaks (or, of course, reads or writes). See also **deep structure**.

survey research A type of **research** involving interviews and questionnaires. One of the main types of survey research is conducted on census data, where it is used to determine the extent of **language maintenance** and **language shift** over time.

syllabic A system of written script in which each character (or **grapheme**) corresponds to a spoken syllable, usually a consonant + vowel pair. Japanese 'kana' is syllabic. See also **Romanisation, writing system**.

syllabus Syllabus and curriculum are sometimes used interchangeably, but there are two ways in which they are distinguished. In the first, curriculum encompasses the totality of the teaching provision in a school or college or educational system, while syllabus refers to the content of one subject, its grading and **assessment** and sometimes too its **methodology**. In the second, curriculum refers to the range of courses offered in one subject, for example, Applied Linguistics, its content, philosophy, specific purposes and **assessment** criteria, while syllabus refers to the content of one component (in this case, of Applied Linguistics), for example, **SLAR**, listing the topics and the readings for each session.

syntax Often used in free variation with **grammar**, but also used to distinguish the study of sentence structure (syntax) from that of word structure (morphology).

systemic functional linguistics A functional model of language, developed by Halliday, which sees language as part of the wider sociocultural context, as social-semiotic. **Grammar** is viewed as **meaning** potential, and the model provides a theory of **text** analysis and **genre**. The model has been influential in (high school) **education** and in applied computing, both because of its social concerns and because it offers a **methodology** for linking language events, at all levels of analysis. It is probably true to say that Halliday has been far more highly regarded by language teachers and educators, especially those involved in teaching the **mother tongue** (or first language) in schools, than by his fellow linguists. His fundamental view of language as socially constructed led to a form of text analysis based on uncovering the hidden ideologies that structure the use of language. As such he may be regarded as the progenitor of **critical discourse analysis**, concerned with the hegemonic structures within texts. See also **function**.

☐ T

talk In **ethnomethodology**, talk means the content of speech, what is said and what is not said. In **conversation analysis**, talk is understood to be an occasion when people act out their sociality. The difference between the two approaches is that ethnomethodology is interested in the what of talk and conversation analysis in the how.

target language The language the learner is learning.

task In **language teaching** a task is any activity which is designed to help achieve a specific learning goal. Thus the request to open the window is not in itself a **language learning** task unless its purpose is to elicit the learner's understanding of the **meaning** of the sentence, rather than simply to let more air into the classroom.

teachers of English as a foreign language see **TEFL**

teachers of English as a second language see **TESL**

teachers of English to speakers of other languages see **TESOL**

teaching materials Anything that is used for teaching (or indeed for learning) a language other than the teacher himself or herself. The term is therefore very broad and includes **texts**, (text)books, other written documents, audio, visual and computer materials (including the internet); indeed anything which, although it may not have been produced with teaching in mind, is used for teaching.

teaching of English as a foreign language see **TEFL**

teaching of English as a second language see **TESL**

technology While **teaching materials** concern what may be loosely called software, technology refers to the hardware and ranges from tape recorders to audiovisual equipment to television, computers and (mobile) telephones. Increasingly, teaching and testing materials are being developed for electronic presentation. See also **CALL**.

TEEP Test of English for Educational Purposes. Designed by Cyril Weir for the former Associated Examining Board in England, the test was designed to be communicative, with a focus on the academic English needed for academic study in the UK. See **communicative language teaching**.

TEFL Teaching (or teachers) of English as a foreign language. English is regarded as a foreign language when it is not the **medium of instruction** in **education** and is not normally used in daily life outside the classroom.

TESL Teaching (or teachers) of English as a second language. English is regarded as a second language when it is the **medium of instruction** in **education** and/or it is normally used in daily life outside the classroom.

TESOL Teachers of English to speakers of other languages. The largest professional organisation of teachers of English as a foreign language, based in the USA and with branches in a number of countries. It organises an annual congress and many other conferences, and publishes both journals (for example *TESOL Quarterly*) and books. Its purpose is to encourage the professionalisation of the field. See also **profession**.

test item An element of a test which requires a specified form of answer or response: item scores are accumulated to provide a test result.

Test of English as a foreign language see **TOEFL**

Test of English for Educational purposes see **TEEP**

testing The measurement of an individual's language **ability** or **knowledge** against a **norm** or a **criterion**. The norm approach requires that the individual be compared with his or her peers, while the criterion approach means that the individual is compared with a specified level of attainment. In both cases, the assumption is that individuals differ from one another. In recent years **language testing** has played an important part in **applied**

linguistics, offering ways of construing **proficiency** and methods of carrying out **research.**

text Any piece of spoken or of written language. This means that a text may be of any length, from one word (on a roadside sign) to a large book. Views differ on how far the context in which the text occurs needs to be taken into account in its interpretation. Useful **language teaching** texts rely only in part on the background **context,** so that the reader needs to struggle with the **language** of the text in order to achieve understanding.

think-aloud protocols (also **think-aloud procedures**) A technique used to investigate learner strategies, this involves learners thinking aloud while they complete a learning **task.** The researcher records those protocols so as to analyse the processes the learner is engaging in. Think-aloud is said to enrich the researcher's understanding of the learner's **performance** on a task. The technique has also been used to investigate judgements made by raters of writing and speaking tests. See also **learning strategies.**

TOEFL Test of English as a Foreign Language, developed in the early 1960s by a consortium of US universities and for many years managed and administered by the Educational Testing Service, Princeton. TOEFL was developed on structural lines, to which it has remained true until recently; it is now undergoing major revision which will make it more communicative and entirely computer based. For many years TOEFL had the largest number of candidates world-wide but over the last few years it has been overtaken by **IELTS.** The Test of English for International Communication (TOEIC) test is a spin-off of TOEFL and has been even more successful in attracting candidates. See also **proficiency.**

transcription (also **notation**) The written record of an oral event. Transcription may be phonetic or graphic. Phonetic transcription is of two kinds: broad (or phonemic) and narrow (or phonetic). Broad transcription is not as detailed or individually precise as narrow transcription. Graphic transcription is even broader, since it makes use of orthographic representation, a hit-and-miss account of what is said which takes no account of **accent, intonation** or stress and must guess how **dialect** terms are to be represented. This is but the extreme case of the problems all transcription (also called notation) encounters.

transfer Used in learning theory to refer to the carrying over of learned behaviour from one situation to another. The distinction is made between positive transfer, which facilitates learning in a new situation, and the opposite, negative transfer.

transformational grammar A model of **grammar** developed in the 1950s by Chomsky which describes the relationship between the **surface structure** (what one hears or sees) and the **deep structure** (the system of underlying rules), the purpose being to reveal the **knowledge** which a **native speaker** of a language uses in forming grammatical sentences and, by implication, the universal human linguistic ability. See also **structural linguistics**.

translation The process of rendering a text that exists in Lx (the source language) into Ly (the **target language**). A free translation does not closely follow the **grammar**, **style** or organisation of the original but reproduces its general **meaning** and intention. A literal translation attempts a word-by-word representation of the original. Most literary translations are of the free kind. Trans-

lation has affinities to **simplification** since, similarly, the
intention is to make a **text** understandable to a new
audience.

turn-taking Research in **CA** has shown that there are strict
turn-taking rules in ordinary **conversation**. These rules
are robust enough to make breakdown in conversation
quite rare. Both speakers and hearers orient to
transition-relevant places (TRP) where speaker change
can occur. If the current speaker does not select a new
speaker then any other party may (self-)select; otherwise
the current speaker may continue for a further turn. If
at the next TRP the current speaker still continues, the
interaction ceases to be a conversation and becomes a
monologue.

T-V pronouns The T and V stand for the French 'tu' and
'vous', the second person singular and plural personal
pronouns. In French and some other languages this
distinction is a marker of age and status, whereby
both inferiors and intimates are addressed as 'tu'. Traditionally the use of the 'tu' form only takes place
between two people after a long period of association,
the change marked by the request to 'tutoyer' one
another. Nowadays, the distinction appears to be
breaking down, especially among the young, who are
much more likely to use the 'tu' form with one another
on first acquaintance. Scholarly work on politeness, an
important part of cultural understanding, owes much to
the earlier work on the T-V pronouns. See also **culture,
politeness, sociolinguistics**.

type–token ratio A measure of **vocabulary** flexibility which
expresses the ratio or proportion of unique (different)
words (type) to the total number (tokens) of words used

in a **text**. For example, consider the sentence: 'In **writing** we employ a wider range of words than we do in ordinary **conversation**.' Here, the total number of words (tokens) is 15; the words 'in' and 'we' are each used twice and are counted as one type each. The type–token ration is therefore 13:15.

typologies Typologies are ways of categorising languages and language situations. Thus language families (Germanic, Indo-European) are one kind of typology, while for **minority language** situations, the categories 'unique', 'non-unique' and 'local-only' have been proposed. No typology is wholly satisfactory, of course, but what typologies do is to help us understand that while languages and situations are unique they also have many features in common. See also **language distance**.

U

UG Universal Grammar; the theory that all adults possess the 'same' grammatical **competence** whatever actual language(s) they speak. The assumption is that there is a human faculty of **language**. This underlies UG, which, it is claimed, is triggered by the **context** into which the young child is born and by normal development to engineer the acquisition of a particular language. There is lack of agreement as to whether the language learner reverts to his or her UG in acquiring a second language or whether he or she proceeds from **knowledge** of his or her first language. See also **SLAR**.

ultimate attainment The outcome or end point of second language acquisition; other terms having the same meaning are 'final state', 'end state' and 'asymptote'. The assumption is that **second language learners** do not (or cannot) become native-like, cannot become **native speakers**. This has been questioned, since some **exceptional learners** do appear to achieve native-likeness. See also **SLAR**.

Universal Grammar see **UG**

uptake The presentation to the learner of language items, known as **input**, is of little use, it is argued, unless that input has been ingested by the learner and then put to use in language encounters. This is uptake.

urban dialectology Traditionally, dialectologists have studied rural **dialects**, but in recent years Labov and others have focused attention on the dialects of cities. No doubt this is partly because of the increasing populations in cities, but more importantly it also reflects an understanding that language change is more readily (because it is more rapid) observed in urban settings. A similar shift of attention from the village to the city can be seen in anthropological research. See also **secular linguistics.**

usage The way language is actually used; therefore synonymous with **language use**. A narrower use of the term has been proposed (by, for example, Widdowson) whereby 'usage' refers to the **function** of an item in a linguistic system while 'use' refers to its function in a **communication** system. See also **performance.**

use see **language use, usage**

utterance The raw data of speech; what is actually said. Utterances are by their nature fugitive; sentences are therefore idealisations of utterances. The written language (apart from a stream of consciousness) is therefore more sentence-like than utterance-like. Utterances belong to **performance** while sentences belong to **competence**.

V

validity The extent to which an instrument, such as a questionnaire or a survey procedure or most often a test, establishes what it is intended to establish. Test validity is regarded as the quality that most affects the value of a test and is seen to be prior to, though dependent on, **reliability**. A language test is valid to the extent that it embodies an abstract concept such as **proficiency** or **aptitude**. Various approaches to validity have been pursued, such as content, concurrent, construct, predictive and, increasingly, consequential. See also **impact, testing**.

variable An attribute or trait which can take on different values. In experimental studies, a dependent variable is the attribute that is being measured, such as the **achievement** of a group of learners after a period of instruction. The independent variable is the treatment that, it is hypothesised, will influence the outcome. The dependent variable will be measured by, for example, a **language proficiency test**, while the independent variable will be measured by the degree of intervention (in medicine, for example, the drug; in **language teaching**, the number of teaching contact hours). In other words, the independent variable may be regarded as any systematic influence which may have an effect on the dependent variable outcome. In **sociolinguistics**, a (linguistic) variable is the minimal unit of linguistic variation and may be grammatical or lexical, but is more usually phonological. Variable shift is indicative of language change. In British English initial (h) may be regarded as a variable with two variants: /h/ and /0/.

variance A descriptive statistic used to describe the dispersion in a single set of scores of one **variable** and to indicate the extent to which two **language varieties** correlate with one another, as shown by the variance they share. Variance can be derived by squaring the standard deviation of a set of scores.

vernacular The dialect in actual use locally, distinguished from **national** and **standard languages** and from **lingua francas**. Labov considers that the vernacular is the proper object of study in **sociolinguistics** because it is the variety least contaminated by other varieties and by notions of **correctness**. See also **colloquial**.

vocabulary The word-stock of a language (also known, more technically, as **lexis**). The term may also refer to the total number of lexical items in a **language variety** (for example the technical vocabulary of medical English). In language teaching and in other areas of **applied linguistics**, vocabulary figures in procedures such as **word frequency** lists, in **cloze procedures** and in measures of **readability**. A distinction is sometimes made between a learner's active vocabulary (those words that she or he uses) and passive vocabulary (those that she or he understands but does not use productively in her or his own speech). Vocabulary includes words, phrases and idioms.

W

washback The effect of testing on teaching, broadly interpreted. Language test washback may be either positive or negative: in other words, all **tests** have washback. Now increasingly studied under the wider umbrella of **impact**.

White Australia policy Until the 1950s, Australia operated this racist immigration policy, which discriminated against those from non-English-speaking countries and in particular seems to have been developed as an exclusion policy against Chinese migrants. Those seeking entry to Australia in the first half of the nineteenth century were required to take a **dictation** test in a **language** with which they were not familiar. Nowadays that requirement has been revived; heads of families are now tested on a version of the **IELTS** test.

women's language In societies where there is clear societal sex-role differentiation, there is likely to be a women's **language** and a men's language (and also, of course, a common language). The differences may be grammatical, phonological or lexical. In societies where the roles overlap, differences are still observed, not by separate languages but by sex-preferential differences, that is, differences in **language use**: such differences may of course be quite subtle.

word frequency list (also known as the **word frequency count**) The frequency with which a word is used in a **text** or **corpus**. The larger the corpus, the more possible it is to make generalisations about **language use** in general, hence the first 1,000 most frequent, the second 1,000 most frequent etc. Such counts are used in the production of simplified reading materials. Those words most frequently occurring in English are ones such as: is, of, and, the, a, with. These words have such a high functional load (that is, they have multiple meanings) that it is not clear how knowledge of their frequency can help the learner. See also **simplification**.

world English(es) The term has several meanings: (a) the use of English world-wide; (b) the model put forward by Kachru of inner, outer and expanding circles; and (c) perhaps most often, the new Englishes found in the ex-British non-settler colonies such as India, Singapore, Nigeria and the Caribbean. See also **colonial discourse.**

writing The use of a **writing system** to record **language**. While speaking is fugitive, writing is permanent; it is also more conservative than speaking and less prone to change. **Standardisation** is a process that acts on the written language, and it is the written language, especially in its print form, that fosters a sense of nationhood. See also **imagined communities.**

writing system A system of representing in **writing** the sounds, syllables and words of a language. The three main types of writing system each focuses on one of these elements: **alphabetic** (sounds), **syllabic** (syllables), **ideographic** (words).

Short Reading List

Dictionaries and encyclopedias

Johnson, Keith and Johnson, Helen (eds), *Encyclopedic Dictionary of Applied Linguistics*, Oxford: Blackwell, 1998.

Richards, Jack C., Platt, John and Platt, Heidi, *Longman Dictionary of Language Teaching and Applied Linguistics*, Harlow: Longman, 1993.

Handbooks

Davies, Alan and Elder, Catherine (eds), *The Handbook of Applied Linguistics*, Oxford: Blackwell, 2004.

Kaplan, Robert B. (ed.), *The Oxford Handbook of Applied Linguistics*, Oxford: Oxford University Press, 2002.

Spolsky, Bernard (ed.), *Concise Encyclopedia of Educational Linguistics*, Oxford: Pergamon/Elsevier, 1999.

Introductions

Allen, J., Patrick, B., Corder, S. Pit and Davies, Alan (eds), *The Edinburgh Course in Applied Linguistics*: volumes 1–4, London: Oxford University Press, 1973–7.

Cook, Guy, *Applied Linguistics*, Oxford: Oxford University Press, 2003.

Davies, Alan, *An Introduction to Applied Linguistics*, Edinburgh: Edinburgh University Press, 1999. (This is the first in the series 'Edinburgh Textbooks in Applied Linguistics': five volumes have so far been published.)

Grabe, William (ed.), 'Applied linguistics as an emerging discipline', *Annual Review of Applied Linguistics*, 2000: 20.

Grabe, William and Kaplan, Robert (eds), *Introduction to Applied Linguistics*, Reading, MA: Addison Wesley, 1991.

Miseka Tomic, Olga and Shuy, Roger W., *The Relation of Theoretical and Applied Linguistics*, New York: Plenum, 1987.

Schmitt, Norbert (ed.), *An Introduction to Applied Linguistics*, London: Arnold, 2002.

Journals

Annual Review of Applied Linguistics, 1979–, Cambridge: Cambridge University Press.

Applied Linguistics, 1980–, Oxford: Oxford University Press.

International Journal of Applied Linguistics, 1991– , Oslo: Novus.

In addition, applied linguistics is now well served by a wide range of specialist material in language testing, second language acquisition research, discourse analysis and so on.